SPORTY'S®

WHAT YOU SHOULD KNOW® SERIES

INSTRUMENT RATING TRAINING COURSE OUTLINE

(FLIGHT TRAINING SYLLABUS)

Sporty's Academy, Inc.
Clermont County/Sporty's Airport
Batavia, OH 45103

© 1995, 2011 by Sporty's Academy, Inc.
All Rights Reserved
Printed in the United States of America
ISBN 978-0-9715631-6-0

For additional copies reorder #M377A

Call: 1 (USA) 800.SPORTYS
(776.7897)

Fax: 1 (USA) 800.359.7794
1 (USA) 513.735.9200

sportys.com

(Intentionally Left Blank)

TRAINING COURSE OUTLINE
INSTRUMENT RATING - AIRPLANE

COURSE OBJECTIVES

The student will obtain the aeronautical skill and experience necessary to meet the requirements for an Airplane Category Instrument Rating.

COURSE COMPLETION STANDARDS

The student must demonstrate through flight tests and school records that the aeronautical skill and experience requirements necessary to obtain an Airplane Category Instrument Rating have been met.

TRAINING COURSE OUTLINE
INSTRUMENT RATING - AIRPLANE

COURSE INTRODUCTION

Sporty's Training Course Outline for the Instrument Rating – Airplane is the syllabus portion of the Sporty's Academy 14 CFR Part 141* Approved Instrument Rating Training Course. This outline provides a logical, structured sequence that maximizes learning and meets 14 CFR Part 141 training time requirements. Training times must be increased slightly to meet 14 CFR Part 61* requirements for students training under those rules. This Training Course Outline also contains ground lessons appropriate to the Instrument Rating.

COURSE CONCEPT

The Instrument Rating course utilizes the building-block theory of learning, which recognizes that each item taught must be presented on the basis of previously learned knowledge and skills.

For optimum effectiveness, the ground lessons and viewing of the associated video segments should be completed prior to the respective flight lessons. If a considerable length of time has elapsed between the ground lesson and the associated flight, the instructor may wish to conduct a short review of essential material.

COURSE ELEMENTS

The course includes the latest FAA pilot certification requirements and a maximum of student-oriented instruction. The syllabus and support materials not only provide necessary information, but also guide the student through the course in a logical manner.

STUDENT VIDEO PREPARATION

The Sporty's Instrument Rating Training Course Outline is based on Sporty's Complete Flight Training course for the Instrument Rating on DVD. It is important that the student view all seven DVDs in the Instrument course. For each ground and flight lesson, there is required review of specific video sections, and this should be accomplished as part of a self-study program. Additional topics may also be assigned by the instructor. To maximize the learning benefit of the DVDs, the student should also review the video sections after completion of the lesson. This is particularly true of any subject areas where the student encountered difficulty.

PREFLIGHT ORIENTATION

Prior to each dual lesson, the instructor must provide the student with a thorough overview of the subject matter to be covered during the lesson. The instructor should select a quiet, private place to brief the student and explain the lesson material. It is important that the instructor define unfamiliar terms and explain the maneuvers and objectives of each lesson.

*14 CFR Part 141 and 14 CFR Part 61 refer to the appropriate parts of Title 14 of the Code of Federal Regulations. Title 14 covers aeronautics and space. The regulations in this title are often referred to as the Federal Aviation Regulations or FARs.

FLIGHT TRAINING DEVICE

Sporty's Training Course Outline for the Instrument Rating is designed to allow practice of maneuvers and procedures in the airplane only after the student has been introduced to and taught the maneuver or procedure in an approved flight training device. Flight training device lessons are more effective for initial explanation, discussion, and introduction of new material. The best results are obtained when the student learns a maneuver or procedure prior to flying the airplane. Ideally the airplane should be used to practice what has been learned in the flight training device. If a flight training device is not available the "(FTD)" lessons can be accomplished in the airplane. When procedures and maneuvers are introduced in the airplane the instructor must explain and discuss the new material to insure that the student thoroughly understands the new material.

AIRPLANE PRACTICE

Airplane practice must be conducted so that the student obtains the maximum benefit from each flight. Each flight, where applicable, should begin with a review of previously practiced maneuvers, as deemed necessary by the instructor, before any new maneuvers are reviewed. If the airplane is not equipped for all of the tasks detailed in a particular lesson, the items that cannot be completed for this reason should be discussed. If there is a possibility that the student will use an airplane that is equipped for these tasks during the practical test, the tasks should be successfully demonstrated by the student at some point in the training.

POSTFLIGHT EVALUATION

The postflight evaluation is equally as important as the preflight orientation. During each postflight session, the student must be thoroughly debriefed. Noticeable advancement should be apparent and recommendations should be made for improvement, where appropriate. This action is a valuable instructional technique because it increases retention. The instructor must also discuss the elements of the next lesson. This prepares the student for the video assignment and will enhance the student's understanding.

LESSON TIMES

Lesson times are specified as a guide to meeting the 14 CFR Part 141 training requirements for the Instrument Rating. Under the building block concept, however, the student must achieve a specific level of proficiency before starting the next lesson. Lessons may be combined or repeated as needed based on the progress made by the student. The Course Time Allocation Table is provided for planning purposes. It is imperative that the instructor and student periodically review the student's overall progress and determine that the training requirements are consistently being met.

STUDENT STAGE CHECKS

Stage checks measure the student's accomplishments during each stage of training. This procedure provides close supervision of training and another opinion on the student's progress. An examination of the building-block theory of learning will show that it is extremely important for progress and proficiency to be satisfactory before the student enters a new stage of training. Therefore, the next stage should not begin until the student successfully completes the current stage. Failure to follow this progression may defeat the purpose of the stage check and lead to overall course breakdown.

GRADING

Evaluation is an essential part of the teaching process. The student must be apprised of his or her progress. All instructional flights must be graded in accordance with the following criteria.

Each pilot operation will be evaluated at the completion of each flight.

1 = EXCELLENT	The student demonstrates knowledge or skills with no procedural or mechanical errors and the flight instructor does not provide any assistance
2 = ABOVE AVERAGE	The student demonstrates knowledge or skills that exceed standards. Occasional procedural or mechanical errors are quickly recognized and corrected.
3 = AVERAGE	The student consistently demonstrates knowledge and skills that meet standards with timely recognition of procedural or mechanical errors.
4 = BELOW AVERAGE	The student demonstrates knowledge and skills with difficulty, is slow in recognizing and correcting procedural or mechanical errors.
5 = BELOW ACCEPTABLE STANDARDS	The student does not demonstrate adequate knowledge or skills, is unable to recognize and correct procedural or mechanical errors.
I = INCOMPLETE	The student has not completed the pilot operation listed.

Each lesson will be assigned an overall grade based on the following criteria.

S = SATISFACTORY	The content of the lesson has been completed to the standards outlined in the individual lesson Completion Standards.
U = UNSATISFACTORY	Indicates that all or part of the lesson content was not completed to the standards outlined in the individual lesson Completion Standards. One or more pilot operations graded as a "5" will require an overall grade of unsatisfactory.
I = INCOMPLETE	Indicates the content of the lesson was not completed, but the pilot operations covered were satisfactory. Pilot operations not completed must be indicated with an "I".

GRADING NOTES

1. When a lesson is graded unsatisfactory, only those pilot operations graded as "5" must be repeated to standards during the next lesson.
2. When a lesson is graded incomplete, the pilot operations not performed must be completed prior to attempting the pilot operations for the next lesson.
3. Use the "CRS TOTALS: (F/I/D/FS)" lines within the grading box to total the student's flight, instrument (in the airplane), ground instruction (discussion), and FTD/simulator times in the course after each lesson.

INSTRUMENT FLIGHT PATTERNS

The instrument flight patterns "A" and "B" and associated text on the following pages have been reprinted from AC 61-27C, the Instrument Flying Handbook that preceded FAA-H-8083-15. AC 61-27C is no longer available, but these patterns are still quite useful in developing a pilot's ability to control the aircraft while flying solely by reference to the instruments. Aircraft control is the primary goal of using the flight patterns; the patterns are only a teaching tool for this purpose.

The instrument flight patterns are used in Stage I of this Training Course Outline.

TSA ALIEN FLIGHT STUDENT PROGRAM RECORDS

The TSA mandated Alien Flight Student Program (AFSP) has a number of compliance and record keeping requirements. Refer to the TSA website for details. The inside front cover of this book has a place to record that you have completed the requirements. That line is there to serve as a reminder to complete the TSA mandates but does not meet the documentation requirements.

Per the TSA, an instructor may elect to use an endorsement in the Student's *and* the Instructor's logbooks to document confirmation of a Student's U.S. Citizenship (not allowed for aliens). The Instructor's copy of the record must be kept for at least 5 years. The recommended text of the endorsement is as follows:

> "I certify that [insert student's name] has presented me a [insert type of document presented, such as a U.S. birth certificate or U.S. passport, and the relevant control or sequential number on the document, if any] establishing that [he or she] is a U.S. citizen or national in accordance with 49 CFR 1552.3(h). [Insert date and instructor's signature and CFI number.]"

For details or clarification, refer to the TSA's website.

Pattern "A"

The purpose of both Pattern "A" and Pattern "B" is to further develop the pilot's ability to control the aircraft without deliberate thought. These patterns help prepare the student for the holding patterns and procedure turns he will fly during radio navigation. Initial practice should be on cardinal headings for simplification; however, as proficiency increases the student should be able to accomplish the patterns on any heading. The instructor may make various changes in the patterns, or, the patterns may be flown over a navigational facility, correcting for drift on each leg.

1. *Brief Student Thoroughly Prior to the Flight*

2. *Performance of Maneuver in the Aircraft*
    a. This maneuver should be performed first with all available instruments, then on partial panel.
    b. Start Pattern "A" and demonstrate through the first three turns, then have the student continue.
    c. Timing should start when the clock second hand is on a cardinal point, preferably the 12 o'clock position.
    d. The timing for this pattern is consecutive in that the time for each leg is started when control pressure is applied to recover from the preceding turn.
    e. After recovery from turns, allow sufficient time for the compass card to stop oscillating, then note the heading and correct if necessary. An exception is the 30-second leg. If you note an error in heading here, compensate for it by lengthening or shortening the time allotted for the next turn.

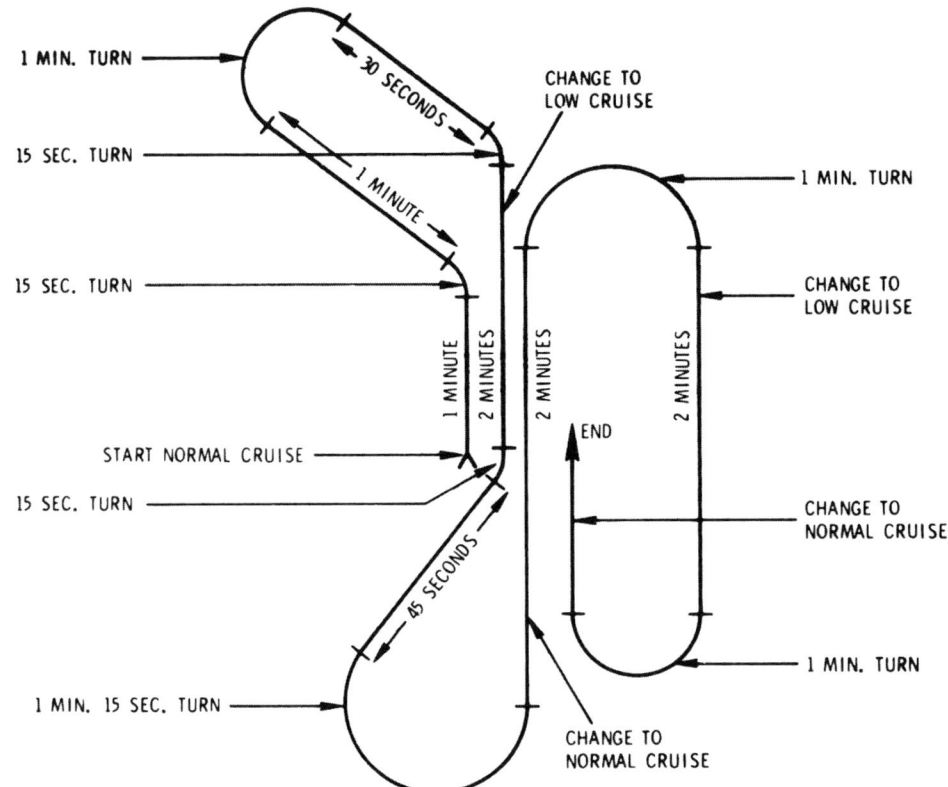

   f. The turn coordinator and magnetic compass must be observed closely at all times. To correct a heading, use a timed turn (for small heading changes, use a half-standard rate turn).
   g. An efficient cross-check is required during airspeed changes so that corrections may be applied immediately.

Pattern "B"

1. *Brief Student Thoroughly Prior to the Flight*
2. *Performance of Maneuver in the Aircraft*
   a. Do not demonstrate unless absolutely necessary.
   b. All available instruments are used.
   c. Roll out on headings regardless of time.
   d. When changing airspeed in turns, *simultaneously* change bank and power, also pitch if applicable.
   e. The descending final turn is made at an absolute rate.
   f. The final descent is made to a minimum altitude set by the instructor, or until the time expires, whichever comes first.
   g. The emergency pull-up is made as a normal go-around procedure, climbing to the original altitude.

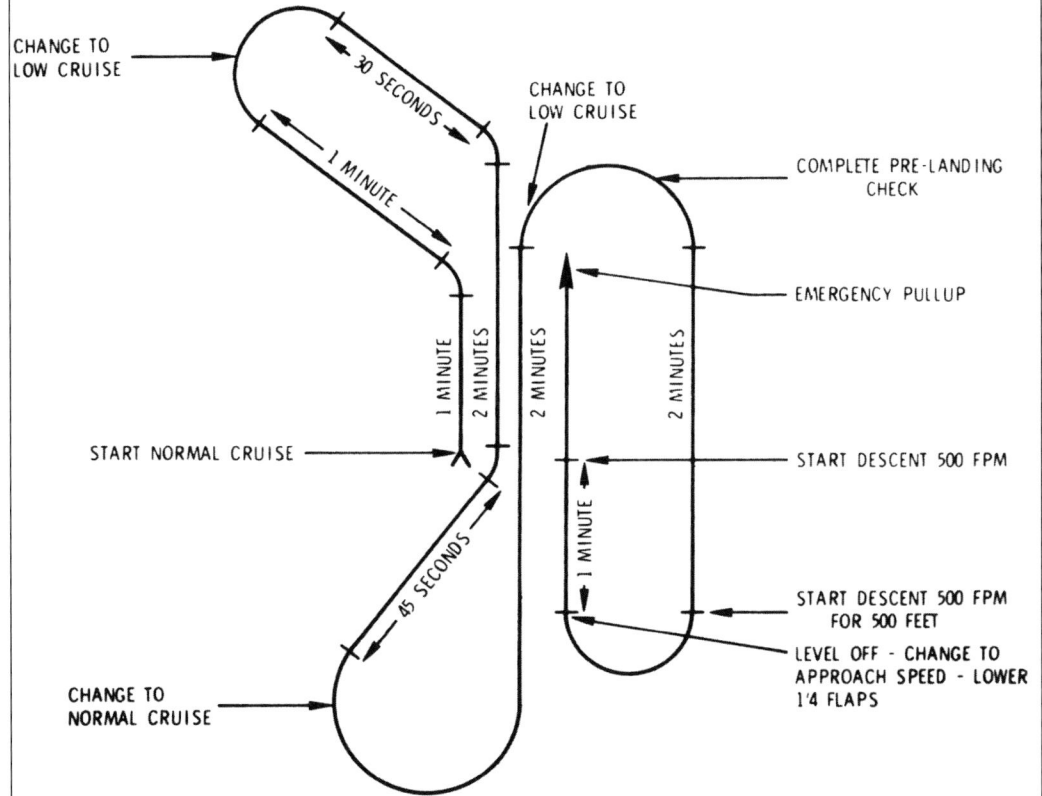

Course Time Allocation Table

STAGE NO.	LESSON	TRAINING TIMES			
		FLT	INSTRUMENT TIME (ACTUAL OR SIMULATED)	FTD	DISCUSSION
I	1				1.2
I	2				1.2
I	3	1.2	1.0		0.4
I	4	1.2	1.0		0.4
I	5	1.2	1.0		0.4
I	6				1.2
I	7	1.2	1.0		0.4
I	8	1.2	1.0		0.4
I	9				1.2
I	10				1.2
I	11			1.5	0.4
I	12	1.2	1.0		0.4
I	13	1.2	1.0		0.4
I	14				1.2
I	15			1.5	0.4
I	16	1.8	1.6		0.4
I	17				1.2
I	18	1.8	1.6		0.4
I - STG CHK	19	1.4	1.2		1.0
STG I TOTALS		13.4	11.4	3.0	13.8
II	20				1.2
II	21			1.5	0.4
II	22				1.2
II	23				1.2
II	24			1.5	0.4
II	25				1.2
II	26	1.8	1.6		0.4
II	27				1.2
II	28				1.2
II	29			1.5	0.4
II	30	2.0	1.8		0.4
II	31				1.2
II	32			1.5	0.4
II	33	2.0	1.8		0.4
II	34				1.2
II	35				1.2
II	36	2.0	1.8		0.4
II	37				1.2
II	38	2.0	1.8		0.4
II - STG CHK	39	2.0	1.8		1.0
STG II TOTALS		11.8	10.6	6.0	16.6
III	40				1.2
III	41				1.2
III	42			2.0	0.4
III	43	3.0	2.8		0.4
III	44			2.0	0.4
III	45	4.0	3.8		0.4
III	46				1.2
III	47	2.0	1.8		0.4
III - STG CHK	48	2.0	1.8		1.0
STG III TOTALS		11.0	10.2	4.0	6.6
COURSE TOTALS		36.2	32.2	13.0	37.0
COMBINED COURSE TOTALS			45.2		
FAA 141 REQUIREMENTS			35.0 TOTAL		30.0 TOTAL

Note: A cross-country flight of at least 250 Nautical Miles along airways or ATC directed routing with one segment of the flight consisting of at least a straight line distance of 100 Nautical Miles between airports is required for Part 141. The flight must involve an instrument approach at each airport and involve 3 different kinds of approaches with the use of navigation systems. Part 61 requires a similar cross-country flight but does not require the 100 miles distance for one segment of the flight.

STAGE I

STAGE OBJECTIVE:

During this stage, the student will learn precise airplane attitude control solely by reference to the airplane instruments.

STAGE COMPLETION STANDARDS:

At the completion of this stage the student will demonstrate precise airplane attitude control by instrument reference only. This will include the use of full panel and partial panel instrument reference. Tolerances for all maneuvers will be in accordance with the Instrument Rating Practical Test Standard.

STAGE I
LESSON 1
DUAL - GROUND
FLIGHT INSTRUMENTS

DATE _____ GRADE (Circle One) S U I

STUDENT NAME _____ STUDENT SIGNATURE _____

INSTRUCTOR # _____ INSTRUCTOR SIGNATURE _____

DISCUSSION: (1.2) _____

CRS TOTALS: (F/I/D/FS) ____ / ____ / ____ / ____

LESSON OBJECTIVE:

During this lesson, the instructor will review the pitot-static and gyroscopic instruments with the student.

CONTENT:

Lesson Introduction

_____ Altimeter
_____ Types of Altitude
_____ Vertical Speed Indicator
_____ Airspeed Indicator
_____ Types of Airspeed
_____ Pitot-Static Instrument Errors

Lesson Introduction

_____ Attitude Indicator
_____ Gyro Driven Heading Indicator
_____ Turn Coordinator / Turn & Bank Indicator
_____ Slip & Skid Indicator
_____ Gyroscopic Instrument Errors
_____ Glass Panel Flight Instrument Displays

COMPLETION STANDARDS:

At the completion of this lesson, the student will have a thorough knowledge of the pitot-static and gyroscopic instruments.

REQUIRED STUDY:

FAA-H-8083-15-IFH - Instrument Flying Handbook
Instrument Rating Practical Test Standards (Refer to Section 1 of the PTS Study Guide, which accompanies Sporty's *Complete* Flight Training Course for the Instrument Rating on DVD.)
Sporty's *Complete* Flight Training Course for the Instrument Rating - DVD Vol 1: Segments 1-14

Notes:

Sporty's *Complete* Flight Training Course — Stage I

STAGE I
LESSON 2
DUAL - GROUND
BAI

DATE_____   GRADE (Circle One) S U I

STUDENT NAME _____ STUDENT SIGNATURE_____

INSTRUCTOR # _____ INSTRUCTOR SIGNATURE_____

DISCUSSION: (1.2) _____

CRS TOTALS: (F/I/D/FS) ____/____/____/____

LESSON OBJECTIVE:

During this lesson, the instructor will introduce the student to concepts related to the control of the aircraft using the aircraft instruments.

CONTENT:

Lesson Introduction

_____ Instrument Scan
_____ Instrument Interpretation
_____ Aircraft Control
_____ Performance Instruments
_____ Control Instruments

Lesson Introduction

_____ Primary Instruments
_____ Supporting Instruments
_____ Direct Indicating Instruments
_____ Indirect Indicating Instruments
_____ Instrument Takeoff

COMPLETION STANDARDS:

At the completion of this lesson, the student will have an understanding of controlling the aircraft by reference to the aircraft instruments.

REQUIRED STUDY:

FAA-H-8083-15-IFH
Instrument Rating Practical Test Standards
Vol 1: Segments 1-14

Notes:
_____
_____
_____
_____
_____

Stage I *What You Should Know*

STAGE I
LESSON 3
DUAL - AIRCRAFT

DATE_____ ACFT/FTD ID_____ GRADE (Circle One) S U I

STUDENT NAME _____ STUDENT SIGNATURE_____

INSTRUCTOR # _____ INSTRUCTOR SIGNATURE_____

FLIGHT TIME: (1.2) _____ DISCUSSION: (0.4) _____

INSTRUMENT: (1.0) _____ CRS TOTALS: (F/I/D/FS) ____/____/____/____

LESSON OBJECTIVE:

During this lesson, the instructor will introduce the student to instrument pre-flight procedures, the instrument cockpit check, the instrument scan, and basic attitude instrument (BAI) flying. The instructor will assist the student in filling out the performance desired table with information for the training aircraft.

CONTENT:

Lesson Introduction

_____ Instrument Preflight and Cockpit Check
_____ Instrument Scan
_____ Instrument Takeoff
_____ Straight-and-Level Flight

Lesson Introduction

_____ Level Standard Rate Turns
_____ Constant Airspeed Climbs
_____ Constant Airspeed Descents
_____ Level-Offs & Trim Use

COMPLETION STANDARDS:

At the completion of this lesson, the student will have a basic knowledge of the instrument preflight procedures, the instrument cockpit check, and the instrument scan.

REQUIRED STUDY:

FAA-H-8083-15-IFH
Instrument Rating Practical Test Standards
Vol 1: Segments 1-5, 9

Performance Desired	Target IAS or VS	Power Setting	Pitch Attitude (Draw on Horizon Line Below)
Straight-and-Level (Low Cruise)			_____
Straight-and-Level (High Cruise)			_____
Cruise Climb			_____
High Performance Climb (Best Rate - V_Y)			_____
Cruise Descent			_____
Low Speed Descent			_____

Notes: _____
_____
_____
_____
_____

Sporty's *Complete* Flight Training Course Stage I

STAGE I
LESSON 4
DUAL - AIRCRAFT

DATE_____ ACFT/FTD ID_____ GRADE (Circle One) S U I

STUDENT NAME _____ STUDENT SIGNATURE_____

INSTRUCTOR # _____ INSTRUCTOR SIGNATURE_____

FLIGHT TIME: (1.2) _____ DISCUSSION: (0.4) _____

INSTRUMENT: (1.0) _____ CRS TOTALS: (F/I/D/FS) ____/____/____/____

LESSON OBJECTIVE:

During this lesson, the instructor will introduce the student to constant rate climbs and descents, steep turns, and climbing and descending turns.

CONTENT:

Lesson Introduction

_____ Constant Rate Climbs/Descents
_____ Climbing/Descending Turns
_____ Steep Turns

Lesson Review

_____ Instrument Preflight
_____ Instrument Cockpit Check
_____ Straight-and-Level
_____ Standard Rate Turns
_____ Constant Airspeed Climbs/Descents
_____ Level-Offs
_____ Instrument Takeoff

COMPLETION STANDARDS:

At the completion of this lesson, the student will be able to perform 45° bank steep turns (180° or 360°) by reference to instruments and have a basic knowledge of constant rate climbs/descents, standard rate turns, and climbing and descending turns. The student will maintain or roll out on assigned headings ±15°, maintain or level off at assigned altitudes ±150', maintain airspeeds ±15 knots, and maintain turning angles of bank ±10°.

REQUIRED STUDY:

FAA-H-8083-15-IFH
Instrument Rating Practical Test Standards
Vol 1: Segments 4-9

Notes:

STAGE I
LESSON 5
DUAL - AIRCRAFT

DATE_____ ACFT/FTD ID_____ GRADE (Circle One) S U I

STUDENT NAME _____ STUDENT SIGNATURE_____

INSTRUCTOR # _____ INSTRUCTOR SIGNATURE_____

FLIGHT TIME: (1.2) _____ DISCUSSION: (0.4) _____

INSTRUMENT: (1.0) _____ CRS TOTALS: (F/I/D/FS) ____/____/____/____

LESSON OBJECTIVE:

During this lesson, the instructor will introduce the student to instrument flight patterns.
Note: Instrument flight patterns are available in the Course Introduction of this book.

CONTENT:

Lesson Introduction

_____ Instrument Flight Patterns

COMPLETION STANDARDS:

At the completion of this lesson, the student will have a basic knowledge of instrument flight patterns. The student will maintain or roll out on assigned headings ±15°, maintain or level off at assigned altitudes ±150', maintain airspeeds ±15 knots, and maintain turning angles of bank ±10°.

REQUIRED STUDY:

FAA-H-8083-15-IFH
Instrument Rating Practical Test Standards
Vol 1: Segments 7-9

Notes:
_____
_____
_____
_____
_____

**STAGE I
LESSON 6
DUAL - GROUND
MAGNETIC COMPASS**

DATE_____   GRADE (Circle One) S U I

STUDENT NAME _____ STUDENT SIGNATURE_____

INSTRUCTOR # _____ INSTRUCTOR SIGNATURE_____

DISCUSSION: (1.2) _____

CRS TOTALS: (F/I/D/FS) ____/____/____/____

LESSON OBJECTIVE:

During this lesson, the instructor will review the magnetic compass with the student

CONTENT:

Lesson Introduction

_____ Magnetic Compass Construction
_____ Principles of Magnetic Attraction
_____ Magnetic Dip
_____ Magnetic Variation
_____ Magnetic Deviation
_____ Northerly Turning Error
_____ Acceleration Error
_____ Oscillation Error

Lesson Introduction

_____ Turns to Magnetic Compass Headings
_____ Calibrating Turn Coordinator
_____ Timed Turns
_____ Partial Panel Instrument Flight
_____ Unusual Attitude Recoveries - Full Panel
_____ Unusual Attitude Recoveries - Partial Panel
_____ Aeromedical Factors for IFR Flight

COMPLETION STANDARDS:

At the completion of this lesson, the student will have a thorough knowledge of the magnetic compass.

REQUIRED STUDY:

FAA-H-8083-15-IFH
Instrument Rating Practical Test Standards
Vol 1: Segments 9-14

Notes:

STAGE I
LESSON 7
DUAL - AIRCRAFT

DATE_____ ACFT/FTD ID_____ GRADE (Circle One) S U I

STUDENT NAME _____ STUDENT SIGNATURE_____

INSTRUCTOR # _____ INSTRUCTOR SIGNATURE_____

FLIGHT TIME: (1.2) _____ DISCUSSION: (0.4) _____

INSTRUMENT: (1.0) _____ CRS TOTALS: (F/I/D/FS) _____/_____/_____/_____

LESSON OBJECTIVE:

During this lesson, the instructor will introduce the student to magnetic compass turns, timed turns, and partial panel instrument flight.

CONTENT:

Lesson Introduction

_____ Magnetic Compass Turns
_____ Partial Panel Instrument Flight
_____ Timed Turns

Lesson Review

_____ Instrument Flight Patterns

COMPLETION STANDARDS:

At the completion of this lesson, the student will have a basic knowledge of magnetic compass turns, timed turns, and partial panel instrument flight. The student will maintain or roll out on assigned headings ±15°, maintain or level off at assigned altitudes ±150', maintain airspeeds ±15 knots, and maintain turning angles of bank ±10°.

REQUIRED STUDY:

FAA-H-8083-15-IFH
Instrument Rating Practical Test Standards
Vol 1: Segments 9-11

Notes:

Sporty's *Complete* Flight Training Course   Stage I

STAGE I
LESSON 8
DUAL - AIRCRAFT

DATE_____ ACFT/FTD ID_____ GRADE (Circle One) S U I

STUDENT NAME _____ STUDENT SIGNATURE_____

INSTRUCTOR # _____ INSTRUCTOR SIGNATURE_____

FLIGHT TIME: (1.2) _____ DISCUSSION: (0.4) _____

INSTRUMENT: (1.0) _____ CRS TOTALS: (F/I/D/FS) ____/____/____/____

LESSON OBJECTIVE:

During this lesson, the instructor will introduce the student to unusual attitude recoveries.

CONTENT:

Lesson Introduction

_____ Unusual Attitude Recoveries - Full Panel
_____ Unusual Attitude Recoveries - Partial Panel

Lesson Review

_____ Instrument Flight Patterns
_____ Partial Panel Instrument Flight

COMPLETION STANDARDS:

At the completion of this lesson, the student will have a basic knowledge of unusual attitude recoveries. During partial panel instrument flight, the student will maintain or roll out on assigned headings ±15°, maintain or level off at assigned altitudes ±150', maintain airspeeds ±15 knots, and maintain turning angles of bank ±10°. During full panel instrument flight maneuvers, the student will maintain or roll out on assigned headings ±10°, maintain or level off at assigned altitudes ±100', maintain airspeeds ±10 knots, and maintain turning angles of bank ±5°.

REQUIRED STUDY:

FAA-H-8083-15-IFH
Instrument Rating Practical Test Standards
Vol 1: Segments 11-14

Notes:
_____
_____
_____
_____
_____

STAGE I
LESSON 9
DUAL - GROUND
NDB FUNDAMENTALS

DATE _____ GRADE (Circle One) S U I

STUDENT NAME _____ STUDENT SIGNATURE _____

INSTRUCTOR # _____ INSTRUCTOR SIGNATURE _____

DISCUSSION: (1.2) _____

CRS TOTALS: (F/I/D/FS) ____ / ____ / ____ / ____

LESSON OBJECTIVE:

During this lesson, the instructor will discuss NDB fundamentals with the student.

CONTENT:

Lesson Introduction

_____ NDB Principles of Operation
_____ NDB Transmitter
_____ ADF
_____ Types of NDBs & Service Volumes
_____ NDB Errors & Irregularities
_____ NDB Tuning, Identifying, and Monitoring

Lesson Introduction

_____ NDB Orientation, Position and Station Passage
_____ Intercepting NDB Bearings
_____ Tracking NDB Bearings / Wind Correction Techniques

COMPLETION STANDARDS:

At the completion of this lesson, the student will have a thorough knowledge of the NDB and its operating principles. The student will also be able to accurately describe the proper techniques for orientation, intercepting, and tracking an NDB bearing.

REQUIRED STUDY:

FAA-H-8083-15-IFH
AIM - Aeronautical Information Manual
Instrument Rating Practical Test Standards
Vol 3: Segments 11-12

Notes:

Sporty's *Complete* Flight Training Course   Stage I

STAGE I
LESSON 10
DUAL - GROUND
VOR FUNDAMENTALS

DATE_____   GRADE (Circle One) S U I

STUDENT NAME _____ STUDENT SIGNATURE_____

INSTRUCTOR # _____ INSTRUCTOR SIGNATURE_____

DISCUSSION: (1.2) _____

CRS TOTALS: (F/I/D/FS) ____/____/____/____

LESSON OBJECTIVE:

During this lesson, the instructor will discuss VOR fundamentals with the student.

CONTENT:

Lesson Introduction

_____ VOR Principles of Operation
_____ VOR Transmitter
_____ VOR Receiving Equipment
_____ VOR Receiver Accuracy Check
_____ VOR Class Designations & Service Volumes
_____ VOR Errors & Irregularities

Lesson Introduction

_____ VOR Tuning and Identifying
_____ VOR Orientation
_____ VOR Intercepting
_____ VOR Tracking / Wind Correction Techniques
_____ VOR Station Passage

COMPLETION STANDARDS:

At the completion of this lesson, the student will have a thorough knowledge of the VOR and its operating principles. The student will also be able to accurately describe the proper techniques for orientation, intercepting, and tracking a VOR radial and also performing a VOR receiver check.

REQUIRED STUDY:

FAA-H-8083-15-IFH
AIM
Instrument Rating Practical Test Standards
Vol 3: Segment 9

Notes:
_____
_____
_____
_____

Stage I — *What You Should Know*

STAGE I
LESSON 11
DUAL - FTD

DATE_____ ACFT/FTD ID_____ GRADE (Circle One) S U I

STUDENT NAME _____ STUDENT SIGNATURE_____

INSTRUCTOR # _____ INSTRUCTOR SIGNATURE_____

FTD/SIM: (1.5) _____ DISCUSSION: (0.4) _____

CRS TOTALS: (F/I/D/FS) _____ / _____ / _____ / _____

LESSON OBJECTIVE:

During this lesson, the instructor will introduce NDB and VOR procedures in the FTD.

CONTENT:

Lesson Introduction

_____ NDB Tuning, Identifying, and Monitoring
_____ NDB Orientation, Position, and Station Passage
_____ NDB Intercepting and Tracking Procedures / Wind Correction Techniques

Lesson Introduction

_____ VOR Tuning and Identifying
_____ VOR Orientation, Position, and Station Passage
_____ VOR Radial Intercepting and Tracking Procedures / Wind Correction Techniques

COMPLETION STANDARDS:

At the completion of this lesson, the student will have a basic knowledge of NDB and VOR procedures. The student will maintain or roll out on assigned headings ±10°, maintain or level off at assigned altitudes ±100', maintain airspeeds ±10 knots, and maintain turning angles of bank ±5°.

REQUIRED STUDY:

FAA-H-8083-15-IFH
Instrument Rating Practical Test Standards
Vol 3: Segments 9 & 11

Notes:
_____
_____
_____
_____
_____

STAGE I
LESSON 12
DUAL - AIRCRAFT

DATE_____ ACFT/FTD ID_____ GRADE (Circle One) S U I

STUDENT NAME _____ STUDENT SIGNATURE_____

INSTRUCTOR # _____ INSTRUCTOR SIGNATURE_____

FLIGHT TIME: (1.2) _____ DISCUSSION: (0.4) _____

INSTRUMENT: (1.0) _____ CRS TOTALS: (F/I/D/FS) ____/____/____/____

LESSON OBJECTIVE:

During this lesson, the instructor will introduce NDB procedures in the training aircraft.
Note: If an airplane with an ADF is not available at the flight school, this lesson may be discarded while still meeting the training requirements of Parts 61 and 141. For Part 141 training operations, the Chief Instructor must sign-off on discarding this lesson.

CONTENT:

Lesson Introduction

_____ NDB Tuning, Identifying, and Monitoring
_____ NDB Orientation, Position, and Station Passage

Lesson Introduction

_____ NDB Intercepting and Tracking Procedures / Wind Correction Techniques

COMPLETION STANDARDS:

At the completion of this lesson, the student will have a basic knowledge of NDB procedures. The student will maintain or roll out on assigned headings ±10°, maintain or level off at assigned altitudes ±100', maintain airspeeds ±10 knots, and maintain turning angles of bank ±5°. While tracking a specified NDB course, the student will apply proper correction to maintain the course, allowing no more than ±20° of deviation.

REQUIRED STUDY:

FAA-H-8083-15-IFH
Instrument Rating Practical Test Standards
Vol 3: Segments 11-12

Notes:
_____
_____
_____
_____
_____

Stage I   *What You Should Know*

STAGE I
LESSON 13
DUAL - AIRCRAFT

DATE_____ ACFT/FTD ID_____ GRADE (Circle One) S U I

STUDENT NAME _____ STUDENT SIGNATURE_____

INSTRUCTOR # _____ INSTRUCTOR SIGNATURE_____

FLIGHT TIME: (1.2) _____ DISCUSSION: (0.4) _____

INSTRUMENT: (1.0) _____ CRS TOTALS: (F/I/D/FS) ____/____/____/____

LESSON OBJECTIVE:

During this lesson, the instructor will introduce the student to VOR procedures and review NDB procedures in the training aircraft.

CONTENT:

Lesson Introduction

_____ VOR Tuning and Identifying
_____ VOR Orientation, Position, and Station Passage
_____ VOR Radial Intercepting and Tracking Procedures / Wind Correction Techniques
_____ Instrument Flight Patterns while Tracking To or From a VOR on a Specified Radial

Lesson Review

_____ NDB Procedures

COMPLETION STANDARDS:

At the completion of this lesson, the student will have a basic knowledge of VOR and NDB procedures. The student will maintain or roll out on assigned headings ±10°, maintain or level off at assigned altitudes ±100', maintain airspeeds ±10 knots, and maintain turning angles of bank ±5°. While tracking a specified VOR course, the student will apply proper correction to maintain the course, allowing no more than 3/4 scale deviation on the CDI.

REQUIRED STUDY:

FAA-H-8083-15-IFH
Instrument Rating Practical Test Standards
Vol 1: Review Segments as Needed
Vol 3: Segments 9 & 11

Notes: _____
_____
_____
_____
_____

Sporty's *Complete* Flight Training Course   Stage I

STAGE I
LESSON 14
DUAL - GROUND
GPS / AUTOPILOT
PRINCIPLES

DATE_____   GRADE (Circle One) S U I

STUDENT NAME _____ STUDENT SIGNATURE_____

INSTRUCTOR # _____ INSTRUCTOR SIGNATURE_____

DISCUSSION: (1.2) _____

CRS TOTALS: (F/I/D/FS) ____/____/____/____

LESSON OBJECTIVE:

During this lesson, the instructor will discuss the principles of GPS and autopilot operation.

CONTENT:

Lesson Introduction

_____ GPS Principles of Operation
_____ Receiver Autonomous Integrity Monitoring (RAIM)
_____ GPS Errors & Irregularities
_____ Wide Area Augmentation System (WAAS)
_____ GPS Modes of Operation
_____ GPS Use Under IFR
_____ GPS CDI Scaling (En Route, Terminal, & Approach)
_____ GPS Waypoints
_____ GPS Direct-To Operations
_____ GPS Flight Plan Operations
_____ GPS Nearest Functions

Lesson Introduction

_____ Substitution of GPS for Other Navigation Radios Under IFR
_____ Orientation, Position, and Waypoint Passage / Sequencing
_____ GPS Course Intercepting and Tracking Procedures / Wind Correction Techniques
_____ Computer Based GPS Procedures Simulator (from Appropriate GPS Manufacturer)
_____ Autopilot Principles of Operation
_____ Autopilot Errors & Irregularities
_____ Autopilot Disconnect Options

COMPLETION STANDARDS:

At the completion of this lesson, the student will have knowledge of GPS and autopilot operation.

REQUIRED STUDY:

FAA-H-8083-15-IFH
AIM
Appropriate Manuals for the Installed GPS & Autopilot
Instrument Rating Practical Test Standards
Vol 6: Segments 5 & 13

Notes:
_____
_____
_____
_____
_____

STAGE I
LESSON 15
DUAL - FTD

DATE_____ ACFT/FTD ID_____ GRADE (Circle One) S U I

STUDENT NAME_____ STUDENT SIGNATURE_____

INSTRUCTOR #_____ INSTRUCTOR SIGNATURE_____

FTD/SIM: (1.5) _____ DISCUSSION: (0.4) _____

CRS TOTALS: (F/I/D/FS) ____/____/____/____

LESSON OBJECTIVE:

During this lesson, the instructor will introduce the student to GPS procedures in the FTD. NDB and VOR procedures will be reviewed as needed.

CONTENT:

Lesson Introduction

_____ GPS Direct-To Operations
_____ GPS Flight Plan Operations
_____ GPS Nearest Functions
_____ GPS Orientation, Position, and Waypoint Passage / Sequencing
_____ GPS Course Intercepting and Tracking Procedures / Wind Correction Techniques

Lesson Review

_____ NDB Procedures
_____ VOR Procedures

COMPLETION STANDARDS:

At the completion of this lesson, the student will have a working knowledge of GPS, NDB, and VOR procedures. The student will maintain headings ±10°, maintain altitudes ±100', maintain airspeeds ±10 knots, and maintain turning angles of bank ±5°. While tracking a specified course, the student will apply proper correction to maintain the course, allowing no more than 3/4 scale deviation on the CDI or ±20° of deviation on the ADF.

REQUIRED STUDY:

FAA-H-8083-15-IFH
Instrument Rating Practical Test Standards
Vol 6: Segment 13

Notes:
_____
_____
_____
_____
_____

Sporty's *Complete* Flight Training Course   Stage I

STAGE I
LESSON 16
DUAL - AIRCRAFT

DATE_____ ACFT/FTD ID_____ GRADE (Circle One) S U I

STUDENT NAME _____ STUDENT SIGNATURE_____

INSTRUCTOR # _____ INSTRUCTOR SIGNATURE_____

FLIGHT TIME: (1.8) _____ DISCUSSION: (0.4) _____

INSTRUMENT: (1.6) _____ CRS TOTALS: (F/I/D/FS) _____/_____/_____

LESSON OBJECTIVE:

During this lesson, the instructor will introduce the student to GPS and autopilot procedures and review NDB and VOR procedures with the student in the training aircraft.

CONTENT:

Lesson Introduction

_____ GPS Direct-To Operations
_____ GPS Flight Plan Operations
_____ GPS Orientation, Position, and Waypoint Passage / Sequencing
_____ GPS Course Intercepting and Tracking Procedures / Wind Correction Techniques
_____ Autopilot Before Takeoff Checks
_____ Autopilot Wing Leveler, Heading, & Navigation Modes (as appropriate)
_____ Autopilot Climb, Descent, & Altitude Hold Modes (as appropriate)
_____ Autopilot Mode Transitions
_____ Autopilot Disconnect Options
_____ Instrument Flight Patterns with the Autopilot

Lesson Review

_____ NDB Procedures
_____ VOR Procedures
_____ Partial Panel Instrument Flight

COMPLETION STANDARDS:

At the completion of this lesson, the student will have a working knowledge of NDB and VOR procedures, and have a basic knowledge of GPS and autopilot procedures. The student will maintain headings ±10°, maintain altitudes ±100', maintain airspeeds ±10 knots, and maintain turning angles of bank ±5°. While tracking a specified course, the student will apply proper correction to maintain the course, allowing no more than 3/4 scale deviation on the CDI or ±15° of deviation on the ADF.

REQUIRED STUDY:

FAA-H-8083-15-IFH
Instrument Rating Practical Test Standards
Vol 1: Segment 11
Vol 6: Segments 5 & 13

Notes:
_____
_____
_____
_____
_____

Stage I   *What You Should Know*

STAGE I
LESSON 17
DUAL - GROUND
FAR/AIM

DATE_____   GRADE (Circle One) S U I

STUDENT NAME _____ STUDENT SIGNATURE_____

INSTRUCTOR # _____ INSTRUCTOR SIGNATURE_____

DISCUSSION: (1.2) _____

CRS TOTALS: (F/I/D/FS) ____/____/____/____

LESSON OBJECTIVE:

During this lesson, the instructor will introduce the student to the Federal Aviation Regulations (FARs) contained in 14 CFR and the sections of the Aeronautical Information Manual (AIM) that pertain to instrument flight.

CONTENT:

Lesson Introduction

_____ 14 CFR Regulations - Applicable to IFR Flight
_____   Part 1
_____   Part 43
_____   Part 61
_____   Part 91
_____   Part 97
_____ NTSB 830

Lesson Introduction

_____ AIM - Chapters Applicable to IFR Flight
_____   Chapter 1
_____   Chapter 2
_____   Chapter 3
_____   Chapter 4
_____   Chapter 5
_____   Chapter 6
_____   Chapter 7

COMPLETION STANDARDS:

At the completion of this lesson, the student will have a basic knowledge of the regulations and the sections of the AIM applicable to instrument flight.

REQUIRED STUDY:

FAA-H-8083-15-IFH
FAR - 14 CFR Aviation Regulations
AIM
Instrument Rating Practical Test Standards
Vol 1: Segments 1-2
Vol 7: Segments 1-14

Notes:
_____
_____
_____
_____
_____

Sporty's *Complete* Flight Training Course   Stage I

STAGE I
LESSON 18
DUAL - AIRCRAFT

DATE_____ ACFT/FTD ID_____ GRADE (Circle One) S U I

STUDENT NAME _____ STUDENT SIGNATURE_____

INSTRUCTOR # _____ INSTRUCTOR SIGNATURE_____

FLIGHT TIME: (1.8) _____ DISCUSSION: (0.4) _____

INSTRUMENT: (1.6) _____ CRS TOTALS: (F/I/D/FS) ____/____/____/____

LESSON OBJECTIVE:

During this lesson, the instructor will review NDB, VOR, GPS, and autopilot procedures, steep turns by reference to instruments, instrument flight patterns, and partial panel instrument flight with the student in the training aircraft.

CONTENT:

Lesson Review

_____ Steep Turns
_____ NDB Procedures
_____ VOR Procedures
_____ GPS Procedures
_____ Autopilot Procedures

Lesson Review

_____ Partial Panel Instrument Flight
_____ Instrument Flight Patterns with Autopilot
_____ Instrument Flight Patterns while Tracking
           VOR Radial (without Autopilot)

COMPLETION STANDARDS:

At the completion of this lesson, the student will be able to perform 45° bank steep turns (180° or 360°) by reference to instruments and have a working knowledge of NDB, VOR, GPS, and autopilot procedures. The student will maintain headings ±10°, maintain altitudes ±100', maintain airspeeds ±10 knots, and maintain turning angles of bank ±5°. While tracking a specified course, the student will apply proper correction to maintain the course, allowing no more than 3/4 scale deviation on the CDI or ±10° of deviation on the ADF.

REQUIRED STUDY:

FAA-H-8083-15-IFH
Instrument Rating Practical Test Standards
Vol 1: Review Segments as Needed
Vol 6: Segments 5 & 13

Notes:
_____
_____
_____
_____
_____

Stage I — *What You Should Know*

PRE-STAGE CHECK – TIME SUMMARY

This page is intended to be used by the student's flight instructor to summarize the times accumulated through this course of instruction and determine that the times are sufficient for the stage requirements. The check instructor should verify that these times are acceptable for completion of the stage.

Part 141 Note: The instrument time in an approved FTD used to meet the minimum requirements of Part 141 may not exceed 40% of the total instrument time required for the course of instruction. This limit is raised to 50% for an approved flight simulator or a combination of an FTD and a simulator.

DATE_____ STUDENT NAME _____ STUDENT SIGNATURE_____

INSTRUCTOR # _____ INSTRUCTOR SIGNATURE_____

STAGE TOTALS

FLIGHT TIME: _____ (In stage only.)

GROUND/DISCUSSION: _____ (Be sure to include the Ground Lesson times.)

FTD/SIM: _____ (In stage only.)

INSTRUMENT: _____ (In flight only.)

STAGE I
LESSON 19
STAGE I CHECK

DATE_____ ACFT/FTD ID_____ GRADE (Circle One) S U I

STUDENT NAME _____ STUDENT SIGNATURE_____

INSTRUCTOR # _____ INSTRUCTOR SIGNATURE_____

FLIGHT TIME: (1.4) _____ DISCUSSION: (1.0) _____

INSTRUMENT: (1.2) _____ CRS TOTALS: (F/I/D/FS) ____/____/____/____

LESSON OBJECTIVE:

This stage check will determine that the student has accomplished the objectives of Stage I.

CONTENT:

Lesson Review

ORAL
_____ Instrument Cockpit Check
_____ Aircraft Systems
_____ Aircraft Flight Instruments
_____ IFR Required Equipment
_____ Inspection Requirements for IFR Flight
_____ Control & Performance Instruments
_____ Primary & Supporting Instruments
_____ Magnetic Compass Errors

Lesson Review

FLIGHT
_____ Instrument Takeoff
_____ Steep Turns
_____ Recovery from Unusual Flight Attitudes
_____ NDB Procedures
_____ VOR Procedures
_____ GPS Procedures
_____ Autopilot Procedures
_____ Partial Panel Instrument Flight

COMPLETION STANDARDS:

At the completion of this lesson, the student will have proficiency in basic attitude instrument flight as well as NDB, VOR, GPS, and autopilot procedures. The student will maintain headings ±10°, maintain altitudes ±100', maintain airspeeds ±10 knots, and maintain turning angles of bank ±5°. While tracking a specified course, the student will apply proper correction to maintain the course, allowing no more than 3/4 scale deviation on the CDI or ±10° of deviation on the ADF.

REQUIRED STUDY:

FAA-H-8083-15-IFH
Instrument Rating Practical Test Standards
Vol 1: Review Segments as Needed
Vol 6: Review Segments as Needed

Notes:

STAGE II

STAGE OBJECTIVE:

During this stage, the student will learn and refine basic radio navigation procedures, including the intercepting and tracking of courses through the use of VORs, Localizers, NDBs and other navigation systems. The student will also learn to perform instrument approaches.

STAGE COMPLETION STANDARDS:

The student will demonstrate positional awareness and the ability to accurately navigate the aircraft by reference to navigation systems. At the completion of this stage the student will be able to perform local instrument flight operations to the current Instrument Rating Practical Test Standards.

Sporty's *Complete* Flight Training Course   Stage II

STAGE II
LESSON 20
DUAL - GROUND
HOLDING & IFR
CLEARANCES

DATE_____   GRADE (Circle One) S U I

STUDENT NAME _____ STUDENT SIGNATURE_____

INSTRUCTOR # _____ INSTRUCTOR SIGNATURE_____

DISCUSSION: (1.2) _____

CRS TOTALS: (F/I/D/FS) ____/____/____/____

LESSON OBJECTIVE:

During this lesson, the instructor will introduce the student to holding and the associated procedures along with IFR clearances.

CONTENT:

Lesson Introduction

- _____ Holding
- _____ Purpose of Holding
- _____ Holding Airspace
- _____ Legs of a Holding Pattern
- _____ Standard vs. Nonstandard Holding Patterns
- _____ Maximum Holding Speeds
- _____ Holding Entry Procedures
- _____ Holding Wind Correction Techniques
- _____ Holding Clearances
- _____ Fix Crossing Check (5T's)

Lesson Introduction

- _____ Timing
- _____ Use of DME while Holding
- _____ Intersection Holding
- _____ Communication Requirements
- _____ Pilot Responsibilities
- _____ ATC Responsibilities
- _____ Elements of an IFR Clearance
- _____ IFR Clearance Compliance, Limits, and Void Times

COMPLETION STANDARDS:

At the completion of this lesson, the student will have an understanding of holding procedures and IFR clearances.

REQUIRED STUDY:

FAA-H-8261-1-IPH - Instrument Procedures Handbook
FAA-H-8083-15-IFH
AIM
Instrument Rating Practical Test Standards
Vol 2: Segments 4-9
Vol 3: Segment 14
Vol 7: Segment 12

Notes:
_____
_____
_____
_____
_____

Stage II — *What You Should Know*

STAGE II
LESSON 21
DUAL - FTD

DATE _____ ACFT/FTD ID _____ GRADE (Circle One) S U I

STUDENT NAME _____ STUDENT SIGNATURE _____

INSTRUCTOR # _____ INSTRUCTOR SIGNATURE _____

FTD/SIM: (1.5) _____ DISCUSSION: (0.4) _____

CRS TOTALS: (F/I/D/FS) ____ / ____ / ____ / ____

LESSON OBJECTIVE:

During this lesson, the instructor will introduce the student to holding procedures, and IFR clearances.

CONTENT:

Lesson Introduction

- _____ Copying / Understanding IFR Clearances
- _____ ATC Communications
- _____ Holding Pattern Entries
- _____ Holding Patterns (VOR/NDB/GPS)

Lesson Introduction

- _____ Fix Crossing Check (5T's)
- _____ Timing
- _____ Use of DME while Holding
- _____ Intersection Holding

COMPLETION STANDARDS:

At the completion of this lesson, the student will have a basic understanding of holding procedures and IFR clearances. The student will maintain headings ±10°, maintain altitudes ±100', maintain airspeeds ±10 knots, and maintain turning angles of bank ±5°. While tracking a specified course, the student will apply proper correction to maintain the course, allowing no more than 3/4 scale deviation on the CDI or ±10° of deviation on the ADF.

REQUIRED STUDY:

FAA-H-8261-1-IPH
FAA-H-8083-15-IFH
Instrument Rating Practical Test Standards
Vol 3: Segment 14
Vol 7: Segment 12

Notes:
_____
_____
_____
_____
_____

Sporty's *Complete* Flight Training Course   Stage II

STAGE II
LESSON 22
DUAL - GROUND
TERMINAL
PROCEDURES

DATE_____ GRADE (Circle One) S U I

STUDENT NAME_____ STUDENT SIGNATURE_____

INSTRUCTOR #_____ INSTRUCTOR SIGNATURE_____

DISCUSSION: (1.2) _____

CRS TOTALS: (F/I/D/FS) ____/____/____/____

LESSON OBJECTIVE:

During this lesson, the instructor will introduce the student to Terminal Procedures Publications.

CONTENT:

Lesson Introduction

_____ Terminal Procedures Publication
_____ Aircraft Approach Categories
_____ Inoperative Components or Visual Aids Table
_____ IFR Take-Off Minimums
_____ Published Departure Procedures
_____ ATC Communication and Compliance with Departure Instructions
_____ Situational Awareness during Departure
_____ Climb & Descent Tables
_____ IFR Alternate Minimums

Lesson Introduction

_____ Radar Instrument Approach Minimums
_____ Pilot Briefing Information Section
_____ Plan View
_____ Profile View
_____ Minimums Section
_____ Airport Sketch & Airport Diagram
_____ Missed Approach Section
_____ Minimum Safe Altitude
_____ Descent Planning
_____ Standard Terminal Arrival Procedures

COMPLETION STANDARDS:

At the completion of this lesson, the student will have an understanding of terminal procedures.

REQUIRED STUDY:

FAA-H-8261-1-IPH
FAA-H-8083-15-IFH
AIM
Instrument Rating Practical Test Standards
Vol 3: Segments 1-3

Notes:
_____
_____
_____
_____
_____

Stage II   What You Should Know

**STAGE II
LESSON 23
DUAL - GROUND
INSTRUMENT
APPROACHES**

DATE_____   GRADE (Circle One) S U I
STUDENT NAME _____ STUDENT SIGNATURE_____
INSTRUCTOR # _____ INSTRUCTOR SIGNATURE_____
DISCUSSION: (1.2) _____
CRS TOTALS: (F/I/D/FS) ____/____/____/____

LESSON OBJECTIVE:

During this lesson, the instructor will introduce the student to various types of instrument approaches without a glideslope.

CONTENT:

Lesson Introduction

_____ Nonprecision Instrument Approaches
_____ Missed Approach Procedures
_____ Timed Approaches
_____ Radar Approaches
_____ Visual Approaches
_____ Contact Approaches
_____ Charted Visual Flight Procedures
_____ Visual Descent Point

Lesson Introduction

_____ Approach Briefing
_____ Circling Approaches
_____ Vectored Approaches
_____ Terminal Arrival Area (TAA) Approaches
_____ Lighting Systems
_____ Visibility Minimums

COMPLETION STANDARDS:

At the completion of this lesson, the student will have an understanding of nonprecision approaches.

REQUIRED STUDY:

FAA-H-8261-1-IPH
FAA-H-8083-15-IFH
AIM
Vol 3: Segments 7-18

Notes:
_____
_____
_____
_____
_____

Sporty's *Complete* Flight Training Course   Stage II

STAGE II
LESSON 24
DUAL - FTD

DATE_____ ACFT/FTD ID_____ GRADE (Circle One) S U I

STUDENT NAME _____ STUDENT SIGNATURE_____

INSTRUCTOR # _____ INSTRUCTOR SIGNATURE_____

FTD/SIM: (1.5) _____ DISCUSSION: (0.4) _____

CRS TOTALS: (F/I/D/FS) _____/_____/_____/_____

LESSON OBJECTIVE:

During this lesson, the instructor will introduce the student to nonprecision approaches and missed approach procedures. Holding procedures will be reviewed.

CONTENT:

Lesson Introduction

_____ Departure Vectors to Filed Route
_____ IFR Navigation
_____ Approach Setup and Briefing
_____ VOR Approach
_____ NDB Approach
_____ GPS Approach (LNAV)
_____ Missed Approach Procedures
_____ Landing from an Approach

Lesson Review

_____ Copying / Understanding IFR Clearances
_____ ATC Communications
_____ Holding Pattern Entries
_____ Holding Patterns (VOR/NDB/GPS)

COMPLETION STANDARDS:

At the completion of this lesson, the student will have a basic understanding of holding procedures, nonprecision approach procedures, and missed approach procedures. The student will maintain headings ±10°, maintain altitudes, other than flight at MDA, ±100', maintain airspeeds ±10 knots, and maintain turning angles of bank ±5°. During nonprecision approaches the student will maintain the MDA, when reached, +200/-0 feet to the MAP and allow no more than a three-quarter-scale deflection of the CDI while on the final approach segment.

REQUIRED STUDY:

FAA-H-8261-1-IPH
FAA-H-8083-15-IFH
Instrument Rating Practical Test Standards
Vol 3: Segments 9-14
Vol 4: Review Segments 1-8 as Needed
Vol 7: Segment 12

Notes:
_____
_____
_____
_____
_____

Stage II *What You Should Know*

STAGE II
LESSON 25
DUAL - GROUND
ATC SYSTEM

DATE_____   GRADE (Circle One) S U I

STUDENT NAME _____ STUDENT SIGNATURE_____

INSTRUCTOR # _____ INSTRUCTOR SIGNATURE_____

DISCUSSION: (1.2) _____

CRS TOTALS: (F/I/D/FS) ____/____/____/____

LESSON OBJECTIVE:

During this lesson, the instructor will introduce the student to the structure of the Air Traffic Control (ATC) system and its applicability to IFR flight.

CONTENT:

Lesson Introduction

_____ Clearance Delivery
_____ Ground Control
_____ Tower Control (Local Control)
_____ Terminal Approach Control Facilities
_____ Approach Control
_____ Departure Control
_____ Final Controller

Lesson Introduction

_____ Air Route Traffic Control Centers (ARTCC)
_____ Tower En Route Control (TEC)
_____ Federal Airways
_____ Uncontrolled Airspace
_____ IFR Flight Planning and Filing Procedures
_____ Closing an IFR Flight Plan

COMPLETION STANDARDS:

At the completion of this lesson, the student will have an understanding of the ATC structure and how it is structured to provide safe and efficient flow of IFR traffic.

REQUIRED STUDY:

FAA-H-8261-1-IPH
FAA-H-8083-15-IFH
AIM
Instrument Rating Practical Test Standards
Vol 2: Segments 1-13
Vol 7: Segment 12

Notes: _____
_____
_____
_____
_____

STAGE II
LESSON 26
DUAL - AIRCRAFT

DATE_____ ACFT/FTD ID_____ GRADE (Circle One) S U I

STUDENT NAME _____ STUDENT SIGNATURE_____

INSTRUCTOR # _____ INSTRUCTOR SIGNATURE_____

FLIGHT TIME: (1.8) _____ DISCUSSION: (0.4) _____

INSTRUMENT: (1.6) _____ CRS TOTALS: (F/I/D/FS) ____/____/____/____

LESSON OBJECTIVE:

During this lesson, the instructor will review IFR navigation, ATC communication procedures, obtaining IFR clearances, performing an approach brief, and executing nonprecision instrument approaches with the student in the training aircraft.

CONTENT:

Lesson Introduction

_____ Filing an IFR Flight Plan
_____ Copying / Understanding IFR Clearances
_____ ATC Communications
_____ Departure Vectors to Filed Route or Pilot Nav to Filed Route
_____ IFR Navigation

Lesson Introduction

_____ Holding Procedures
_____ Approach Setup and Brief
_____ VOR Approach
_____ NDB Approach
_____ GPS Approach (LNAV)
_____ Missed Approach Procedures

COMPLETION STANDARDS:

At the completion of this lesson, the student will be able to navigate, hold en route, and perform VOR, NDB, and GPS approaches with minimal instructor assistance. The student should also be able to perform ATC communications with minimal instructor assistance. The student will maintain headings ±10°, maintain altitudes, other than flight at MDA or during the final approach segment of a precision approach, ±100', maintain airspeeds ±10 knots, and maintain turning angles of bank ±5°. During nonprecision approaches the student will maintain the MDA, when reached, +200/-0 feet to the MAP and allow no more than a three-quarter-scale deflection of the CDI while on the final approach segment.

REQUIRED STUDY:

FAA-H-8261-1-IPH
FAA-H-8083-15-IFH
Instrument Rating Practical Test Standards
Vol 3: Segments 7-13

Notes:
_____
_____
_____
_____
_____

Stage II *What You Should Know*

**STAGE II
LESSON 27
DUAL - GROUND
PILOT / CONTROLLER
RESPONSIBILITIES**

DATE_____ GRADE (Circle One) S U I

STUDENT NAME _____ STUDENT SIGNATURE_____

INSTRUCTOR # _____ INSTRUCTOR SIGNATURE_____

DISCUSSION: (1.2) _____

CRS TOTALS: (F/I/D/FS) ____/____/____/____

LESSON OBJECTIVE:

During this lesson, the instructor will introduce the student to the responsibilities of the Pilot and the Air Traffic Controller.

CONTENT:

Lesson Introduction

_____ Air Traffic Clearance
_____ Contact Approach
_____ Visual Approach
_____ Instrument Approach
_____ Missed Approach
_____ Radar Vectors
_____ Safety Alerts
_____ Speed Adjustments
_____ Visual Separation
_____ Instrument Departures

Lesson Introduction

_____ Wake Turbulence Separations
_____ Compulsory Reporting Points
_____ Loss of Communications
_____ Land and Hold Short Operations
_____ Practice Instrument Approaches
_____ IFR Separation Standards
_____ See and Avoid
_____ Traffic Advisories
_____ VFR-On-Top
_____ Minimum Fuel Advisory

COMPLETION STANDARDS:

At the completion of this lesson, the student will have an understanding of pilot and controller responsibilities.

REQUIRED STUDY:

FAA-H-8261-1-IPH
FAA-H-8083-15-IFH
AIM
Instrument Rating Practical Test Standards
Vol 2: Segments 1-13
Vol 3: Segments 7-8

Notes: _____
_____
_____
_____
_____

Sporty's *Complete* Flight Training Course   Stage II

**STAGE II
LESSON 28
DUAL - GROUND
INSTRUMENT
LANDING SYSTEM**

DATE_____ GRADE (Circle One) S U I

STUDENT NAME _____ STUDENT SIGNATURE_____

INSTRUCTOR # _____ INSTRUCTOR SIGNATURE_____

DISCUSSION: (1.2) _____

CRS TOTALS: (F/I/D/FS) ____/____/____/____

LESSON OBJECTIVE:

During this lesson, the instructor will introduce the instrument landing system and associated approaches to the student. WAAS approaches will also be covered.

CONTENT:

Lesson Introduction

_____ Localizer Principles of Operation
_____ Glideslope Principles of Operation
_____ Marker Beacons
_____ ILS Receiving Equipment
_____ ILS Categories
_____ ILS Errors & Irregularities

Lesson Introduction

_____ Localizer and Glideslope Critical Areas
_____ Simplified Directional Facility
_____ Localizer-Type Directional Aid
_____ Precision Instrument Approaches
_____ Back Course Approaches
_____ APV Instrument Approaches

COMPLETION STANDARDS:

At the completion of this lesson, the student will have a thorough knowledge of the ILS, LDA, SDF, and WAAS systems and their operating principles.

REQUIRED STUDY:

FAA-H-8261-1-IPH
FAA-H-8083-15-IFH
AIM
Instrument Rating Practical Test Standards
Vol 3: Segments 1-5

Notes:
_____
_____
_____
_____
_____

STAGE II
LESSON 29
DUAL - FTD

DATE_____ ACFT/FTD ID_____ GRADE (Circle One) S U I

STUDENT NAME _____ STUDENT SIGNATURE_____

INSTRUCTOR # _____ INSTRUCTOR SIGNATURE_____

FTD/SIM: (1.5) _____ DISCUSSION: (0.4) _____

CRS TOTALS: (F/I/D/FS) ____/____/____/____

LESSON OBJECTIVE:

During this lesson, the instructor will introduce the student to ILS and back course approach procedures.

CONTENT:

Lesson Introduction

_____ ILS Approach (Full & Vectored)
_____ Landing from an ILS Approach
_____ Back Course Approach

Lesson Review

_____ Missed Approach Procedures

COMPLETION STANDARDS:

At the completion of this lesson, the student will have a basic understanding of ILS and back course approach procedures. The student will maintain headings ±10°, maintain altitudes, other than during the final approach segment, ±100', maintain airspeeds ±10 knots, and maintain turning angles of bank ±5°. During precision approaches the student will avoid descents below the DA/DH before initiating a missed approach procedure or transitioning to a normal landing approach and allow no more than a three-quarter-scale deflection of the localizer or glideslope while on the final approach segment.

REQUIRED STUDY:

FAA-H-8261-1-IPH
FAA-H-8083-15-IFH
Instrument Rating Practical Test Standards
Vol 3: Segments 1-5
Vol 4: Segments 9-10

Notes:
_____
_____
_____
_____
_____

STAGE II
LESSON 30
DUAL - AIRCRAFT

DATE_____ ACFT/FTD ID_____ GRADE (Circle One) S U I

STUDENT NAME _____ STUDENT SIGNATURE_____

INSTRUCTOR # _____ INSTRUCTOR SIGNATURE_____

FLIGHT TIME: (2.0) _____ DISCUSSION: (0.4) _____

INSTRUMENT: (1.8) _____ CRS TOTALS: (F/I/D/FS) _____/_____/_____/_____

LESSON OBJECTIVE:

During this lesson, the instructor will introduce the student to ILS, back course, and APV approach procedures in the training aircraft. Holding, VOR and GPS approaches, and missed approach procedures will be reviewed.

CONTENT:

Lesson Introduction

_____ ILS Approach
_____ Back Course Approach
_____ APV Approach (LPV or LNAV/VNAV)

Lesson Review

_____ Filing an IFR Flight Plan
_____ Copying / Understanding IFR Clearances
_____ ATC Communications
_____ IFR Navigation
_____ Holding Procedures
_____ Approach Setup and Brief
_____ VOR Approach
_____ GPS Approach (LNAV)
_____ Missed Approach Procedures

COMPLETION STANDARDS:

At the completion of this lesson, the student will be able to navigate, hold en route, and perform ILS, VOR, and GPS approaches with minimal instructor assistance. The student should also be able to perform ATC communications with minimal instructor assistance. The student will maintain headings ±10°, maintain altitudes, other than flight at MDA or during the final approach segment of a precision approach, ±100', maintain airspeeds ±10 knots, and maintain turning angles of bank ±5°. During nonprecision approaches the student will maintain the MDA, when reached, +200/-0 feet to the MAP and allow no more than a three-quarter-scale deflection of the CDI while on the final approach segment. During precision and APV approaches the student will avoid descents below the DA/DH before initiating a missed approach procedure or transitioning to a normal landing approach and allow no more than a three-quarter-scale deflection of the CDI or glideslope while on the final approach segment.

REQUIRED STUDY:

FAA-H-8261-1-IPH
FAA-H-8083-15-IFH
Instrument Rating Practical Test Standards
Vol 3: Segments 4-13
Vol 6: Segment 13

Notes:

**STAGE II
LESSON 31
DUAL - GROUND
AUTOPILOT
APPROACHES & DME**

DATE_____ GRADE (Circle One) S U I

STUDENT NAME _____ STUDENT SIGNATURE_____

INSTRUCTOR # _____ INSTRUCTOR SIGNATURE_____

DISCUSSION: (1.2) _____

CRS TOTALS: (F/I/D/FS) ____/____/____/____

LESSON OBJECTIVE:

During this lesson, the instructor will introduce the student to distance measuring equipment, the use of the autopilot for approaches, and instrument approaches with loss of primary flight instrument indicators (partial panel).

CONTENT:

Lesson Introduction

_____ Autopilot Approach Operations & Limitations
_____ Nonprecision Approaches with an Autopilot
_____ APV Approaches with an Autopilot
_____ Precision Approaches with an Autopilot
_____ Back Course Approaches with an Autopilot
_____ Missed Approach Procedures with an Autopilot
_____ Holding Procedures with an Autopilot

Lesson Introduction

_____ DME Principles of Operation
_____ DME Errors & Irregularities
_____ DME Arc Interception
_____ DME Arc Tracking
_____ Use of GPS as Substitute for DME
_____ Instrument Approaches with Loss of Primary Flight Instrument Indicators (Partial Panel)

COMPLETION STANDARDS:

At the completion of this lesson, the student will have an understanding of distance measuring equipment, the use of the autopilot for approaches, and partial panel approaches.

REQUIRED STUDY:

FAA-H-8261-1-IPH
FAA-H-8083-15-IFH
AIM
Instrument Rating Practical Test Standards
Vol 3: Segments 16-18
Vol 6: Segments 3-5

Notes:

STAGE II
LESSON 32
DUAL - FTD

DATE_____ ACFT/FTD ID_____ GRADE (Circle One) S U I

STUDENT NAME _____ STUDENT SIGNATURE_____

INSTRUCTOR # _____ INSTRUCTOR SIGNATURE_____

FTD/SIM: (1.5) _____ DISCUSSION: (0.4) _____

CRS TOTALS: (F/I/D/FS) _____ / _____ / _____

LESSON OBJECTIVE:

During this lesson, the instructor will introduce the student to partial panel approaches, DME arcs, and circle to land procedures.

CONTENT:

Lesson Introduction

_____ Nonprecision Approach with Loss of Primary Flight Instrument Indicators (Partial Panel)
_____ Precision Approach with Loss of Primary Flight Instrument Indicators (Partial Panel)

Lesson Introduction

_____ DME Arc
_____ Circle to Land Procedures

COMPLETION STANDARDS:

At the completion of this lesson, the student will be able to perform partial panel VOR approaches, and DME arcs. The student will maintain headings ±10°, maintain altitudes, other than flight at MDA, ±100', maintain airspeeds ±10 knots, and maintain turning angles of bank ±5°. During nonprecision approaches the student will maintain the MDA, when reached, +200/-0 feet to the MAP and allow no more than a three-quarter-scale deflection of the CDI while on the final approach segment.

REQUIRED STUDY:

FAA-H-8261-1-IPH
FAA-H-8083-15-IFH
Instrument Rating Practical Test Standards
Vol 2: Review Segments as Needed
Vol 3: Segments 15-18

Notes:

Stage II　　　　　　　　　　　　　　　　　　　　　　　　　　　　　　　　　　　　　　*What You Should Know*

STAGE II
LESSON 33
DUAL - AIRCRAFT

DATE_____ ACFT/FTD ID_____ GRADE (Circle One) S U I

STUDENT NAME _____ STUDENT SIGNATURE_____

INSTRUCTOR # _____ INSTRUCTOR SIGNATURE_____

　　　　FLIGHT TIME: (2.0) _____ DISCUSSION: (0.4) _____

INSTRUMENT: (1.8) _____ CRS TOTALS: (F/I/D/FS) _____/_____/_____

LESSON OBJECTIVE:

During this lesson, the instructor will review partial panel approaches, DME arcs, nonprecision approaches, precision approaches, and circle to land procedures with the student.

CONTENT:

Lesson Introduction

_____ Nonprecision Approach with Loss of Primary Flight Instrument Indicators (Partial Panel)
_____ APV Approach with Loss of Primary Flight Instrument Indicators (Partial Panel)
_____ Precision Approach with Loss of Primary Flight Instrument Indicators (Partial Panel)
_____ DME Arcs
_____ Circle to Land Procedures

Lesson Review

_____ Nonprecision Approaches - Full & Vectored (Full Panel)
_____ APV Approaches - Full & Vectored (Full Panel)
_____ Precision Approaches - Full & Vectored (Full Panel)

COMPLETION STANDARDS:

At the completion of this lesson, the student will be able to perform nonprecision approaches, precision approaches, circling procedures, and DME arcs with minimal instructor assistance. The student will maintain headings ±10°, maintain altitudes, other than flight at MDA or during the final approach segment of a precision approach, ±100', maintain airspeeds ±10 knots, and maintain turning angles of bank ±5°. During nonprecision approaches the student will maintain the MDA, when reached, +100/-0 feet to the MAP and allow no more than a three-quarter-scale deflection of the CDI while on the final approach segment. During precision and APV approaches the student will avoid descents below the DA/DH before initiating a missed approach procedure or transitioning to a normal landing approach and allow no more than a three-quarter-scale deflection of the CDI or glideslope while on the final approach segment.

REQUIRED STUDY:

FAA-H-8261-1-IPH
FAA-H-8083-15-IFH
Instrument Rating Practical Test Standards
Vol 3: Review Segments as Needed

Notes:

STAGE II
LESSON 34
DUAL - GROUND
ICING

DATE_____ GRADE (Circle One) S U I

STUDENT NAME _____ STUDENT SIGNATURE_____

INSTRUCTOR # _____ INSTRUCTOR SIGNATURE_____

DISCUSSION: (1.2) _____

CRS TOTALS: (F/I/D/FS) ____/____/____/____

LESSON OBJECTIVE:

During this lesson, the instructor will introduce the student to weather conditions associated with icing.

CONTENT:

Lesson Introduction

- _____ Required Conditions for Ice Formation
- _____ Formation of Frost
- _____ Formation of Clear Ice
- _____ Formation of Rime Ice
- _____ Formation of Mixed Ice

Lesson Introduction

- _____ Icing Intensities
- _____ PIREPs Specific to Icing
- _____ AIRMETs Specific to Icing
- _____ SIGMETs Specific to Icing
- _____ Winds / Temps Aloft Forecast

COMPLETION STANDARDS:

At the completion of this lesson, the student will have an understanding of icing associated with IFR flight.

REQUIRED STUDY:

FAA-H-8083-15-IFH
AIM
Instrument Rating Practical Test Standards
AC 00-6-AvWx - Aviation Weather
AC 00-45-AvWxSvc - Aviation Weather Services
Vol 5: Segments 1-5

Notes:

Stage II What You Should Know

**STAGE II
LESSON 35
DUAL - GROUND
THUNDERSTORMS**

DATE_____   GRADE (Circle One) S U I

STUDENT NAME _____ STUDENT SIGNATURE_____

INSTRUCTOR # _____ INSTRUCTOR SIGNATURE_____

DISCUSSION: (1.2) _____

CRS TOTALS: (F/I/D/FS) ____/____/____/____

LESSON OBJECTIVE:

During this lesson, the instructor will introduce the student to thunderstorms and their associated phenomena.

CONTENT:

Lesson Introduction

_____ Conditions Required for Thunderstorms
_____ Thunderstorm Lifecycle
_____ Air Mass Thunderstorms
_____ Steady State Thunderstorms
_____ Squall Line Thunderstorms
_____ Embedded Thunderstorms

Lesson Introduction

_____ Radar Reports / Radar Summary Chart
_____ Frontal Thunderstorms
_____ Hazards Associated with Thunderstorms
_____ Forecasts Associated with Thunderstorms
_____ Convective SIGMETs

COMPLETION STANDARDS:

At the completion of this lesson, the student will have an understanding of thunderstorms and their associated phenomena.

REQUIRED STUDY:

FAA-H-8083-15-IFH
AIM
Instrument Rating Practical Test Standards
AC 00-6-AvWx
AC 00-45-AvWxSvc
Vol 5: Segments 5-14

Notes: _____
_____
_____
_____
_____

Sporty's *Complete* Flight Training Course   Stage II

STAGE II
LESSON 36
DUAL - AIRCRAFT

DATE_____ ACFT/FTD ID_____ GRADE (Circle One) S U I

STUDENT NAME _____ STUDENT SIGNATURE_____

INSTRUCTOR # _____ INSTRUCTOR SIGNATURE_____

FLIGHT TIME: (2.0) _____ DISCUSSION: (0.4) _____

INSTRUMENT: (1.8) _____ CRS TOTALS: (F/I/D/FS) ____/____/____/____

LESSON OBJECTIVE:

During this lesson, the instructor will introduce the student to approaches using the autopilot and review nonprecision, APV, and precision approaches, holding, and missed approach procedures with the student.

CONTENT:

Lesson Introduction

_____ Nonprecision Approach with an Autopilot
_____ APV Approach with an Autopilot
_____ Precision Approach with an Autopilot
_____ Back Course Approach with an Autopilot
_____ Missed Approach Procedures with an Autopilot

Lesson Review

_____ Nonprecision Approach - Full & Vectored (Full & Partial Panel)
_____ APV Approach - Full & Vectored (Full & Partial Panel)
_____ Precision Approach - Full & Vectored (Full & Partial Panel)
_____ Back Course Approach
_____ Holding Procedures
_____ ATC Procedures
_____ Missed Approach Procedures
_____ Circle To Land Procedures

COMPLETION STANDARDS:

At the completion of this lesson, the student will be able to perform instrument approaches with minimal instructor assistance. The student will maintain headings ±10°, maintain altitudes, other than flight at MDA or during the final approach segment of a precision approach, ±100', maintain airspeeds ±10 knots, and maintain turning angles of bank ±5°. During nonprecision approaches the student will maintain the MDA, when reached, +100/-0 feet to the MAP and allow no more than a three-quarter-scale deflection of the CDI while on the final approach segment. During precision and APV approaches the student will avoid descents below the DA/DH before initiating a missed approach procedure or transitioning to a normal landing approach and allow no more than a three-quarter-scale deflection of the CDI or glideslope while on the final approach segment.

REQUIRED STUDY:

FAA-H-8083-15-IFH
Instrument Rating Practical Test Standards
Vol 3: Review Segments as Needed
Vol 6: Segments 3-5

Notes:
_____
_____
_____
_____
_____

Stage II   *What You Should Know*

STAGE II
LESSON 37
DUAL - GROUND
FORECASTS & REPORTS

DATE_____   GRADE (Circle One) S U I
STUDENT NAME _____ STUDENT SIGNATURE_____
INSTRUCTOR # _____ INSTRUCTOR SIGNATURE_____
DISCUSSION: (1.2) _____
CRS TOTALS: (F/I/D/FS) ____/____/____/____

LESSON OBJECTIVE:

During this lesson, the instructor will review weather forecasts with the student.

CONTENT:

Lesson Introduction

_____ Area Forecasts
_____ Terminal Aerodrome Forecasts
_____ METARs
_____ Winds / Temperatures Aloft
_____ Pilot Reports
_____ Radar Reports / Radar Summary Chart
_____ Surface Analysis Chart
_____ Weather Depiction Chart

Lesson Introduction

_____ Freezing Level Chart
_____ Upper Level Charts
_____ Significant Weather Prognostic Charts
_____ Prognostic Chart
_____ SIGMETs, AIRMETs, & Convective SIGMETs
_____ Recognition of Critical Weather Situations
_____ Windshear Avoidance

COMPLETION STANDARDS:

At the completion of this lesson, the student will have a thorough understanding of weather forecasts.

REQUIRED STUDY:

FAA-H-8083-15-IFH
AIM
Instrument Rating Practical Standard
AC 00-6-AvWx
AC 00-45-AvWxSvc
Vol 7: Segments 1-4

Notes:
_____
_____
_____
_____
_____

Sporty's *Complete* Flight Training Course   Stage II

STAGE II
LESSON 38
DUAL - AIRCRAFT

DATE_____ ACFT/FTD ID_____ GRADE (Circle One) S U I

STUDENT NAME _____ STUDENT SIGNATURE_____

INSTRUCTOR # _____ INSTRUCTOR SIGNATURE_____

FLIGHT TIME: (2.0) _____ DISCUSSION: (0.4) _____

INSTRUMENT: (1.8) _____ CRS TOTALS: (F/I/D/FS) ____/____/____/____

LESSON OBJECTIVE:

During this lesson, the instructor will review approaches using the autopilot, nonprecision approaches, APV approaches, precision approaches, holding, and missed approach procedures with the student.

CONTENT:

Lesson Review

_____ Nonprecision Approach with an Autopilot
_____ Precision Approach with an Autopilot
_____ Missed Approach Procedures with an Autopilot
_____ Nonprecision Approach - Full & Vectored (Full & Partial Panel)
_____ APV Approach - Full & Vectored (Full & Partial Panel)

Lesson Review

_____ Precision Approach - Full & Vectored (Full & Partial Panel)
_____ Back Course Approach
_____ Holding Procedures
_____ ATC Communications
_____ Missed Approach Procedures
_____ Circle to Land Procedures

COMPLETION STANDARDS:

At the completion of this lesson, the student will be able to perform instrument approaches with minimal instructor assistance. The student will maintain headings ±10°, maintain altitudes, other than flight at MDA or during the final approach segment of a precision approach, ±100', maintain airspeeds ±10 knots, and maintain turning angles of bank ±5°. During nonprecision approaches the student will maintain the MDA, when reached, +100/-0 feet to the MAP and allow no more than a three-quarter-scale deflection of the CDI while on the final approach segment. During precision and APV approaches the student will avoid descents below the DA/DH before initiating a missed approach procedure or transitioning to a normal landing approach and allow no more than a three-quarter-scale deflection of the CDI or glideslope while on the final approach segment.

REQUIRED STUDY:

FAA-H-8083-15-IFH
Instrument Rating Practical Test Standards
Vol 3: Review Segments as Needed
Vol 4: Segments 11-14
Vol 5: Segments 11-14

Notes:
_____
_____
_____
_____
_____

PRE-STAGE CHECK – TIME SUMMARY

This page is intended to be used by the student's flight instructor to summarize the times accumulated through this course of instruction and determine that the times are sufficient for the stage requirements. The check instructor should verify that these times are acceptable for completion of the stage.

Part 141 Note: The instrument time in an approved FTD used to meet the minimum requirements of Part 141 may not exceed 40% of the total instrument time required for the course of instruction. This limit is raised to 50% for an approved flight simulator or a combination of an FTD and a simulator.

DATE_____ STUDENT NAME _____ STUDENT SIGNATURE_____

INSTRUCTOR # _____ INSTRUCTOR SIGNATURE_____

STAGE TOTALS

FLIGHT TIME: _____ (In stage only.)

GROUND/DISCUSSION: _____ (Be sure to include the Ground Lesson times.)

FTD/SIM: _____ (In stage only.)

INSTRUMENT: _____ (In flight only.)

COURSE TOTALS

FLIGHT TIME: _____ (In course only.)

GROUND/DISCUSSION: _____ (Be sure to include the Ground Lesson times.)

FTD/SIM: _____ (In course only.)

INSTRUMENT: _____ (In flight only.)

Sporty's *Complete* Flight Training Course   Stage II

STAGE II
LESSON 39
STAGE II CHECK

DATE_____ ACFT/FTD ID_____ GRADE (Circle One) S U I

STUDENT NAME _____ STUDENT SIGNATURE_____

INSTRUCTOR # _____ INSTRUCTOR SIGNATURE_____

FLIGHT TIME: (2.0) _____ DISCUSSION: (1.0) _____

INSTRUMENT: (1.8) _____ CRS TOTALS: (F/I/D/FS) ____/____/____/____

LESSON OBJECTIVE:

During this lesson, the student will complete a stage check covering approaches and holding procedures.

CONTENT:

Lesson Review

ORAL

_____ Weather Information
_____ Holding Procedures
_____ Terminal Procedures Publication
_____ Approach Procedures
_____ Published Departure Procedures
_____ Standard Terminal Arrival Procedures
_____ Instrument Approaches with Loss of Primary Flight Instrument Indicators (Partial Panel)

Lesson Review

FLIGHT

_____ ATC Clearances
_____ Clearance Compliance
_____ Holding Procedures
_____ Nonprecision Approach
_____ APV Approach
_____ Precision Approach
_____ Missed Approach Procedures
_____ Nonprecision Approach with Loss of Primary Flight Instrument Indicators
_____ APV Approach with Loss of Primary Flight Instrument Indicators
_____ Precision Approach with Loss of Primary Flight Instrument Indicators
_____ Nonprecision Approach with Autopilot
_____ Missed Approach Procedures with an Autopilot
_____ Circling Approach
_____ Landing from Straight-In / Circling Approach

COMPLETION STANDARDS:

The student shall perform all maneuvers to the standards established by the Instrument Rating Practical Test Standards. The student should demonstrate at least the number of approaches indicated in the PTS. Additional approaches within the capability of the are desirable.

REQUIRED STUDY:

Instrument Rating Practical Test Standards
Vol 1-7: Review Segments as Needed

Notes:
_____
_____
_____
_____
_____

STAGE III

STAGE OBJECTIVE:

During this stage, the student will plan and perform IFR cross-country flights while refining the basic IFR skills required to operate in the instrument environment.

STAGE COMPLETION STANDARDS:

The student will demonstrate positional awareness and the ability to accurately navigate the aircraft by reference to navigation systems. At the completion of this stage the student will be able to perform instrument flight operations to the current Instrument Rating Practical Test Standards.

**STAGE III
LESSON 40
DUAL - GROUND
CHART REVIEW &
EN ROUTE PROCEDURES**

DATE_____ GRADE (Circle One) S U I

STUDENT NAME _____ STUDENT SIGNATURE_____

INSTRUCTOR # _____ INSTRUCTOR SIGNATURE_____

DISCUSSION: (1.2) _____

CRS TOTALS: (F/I/D/FS) ____/____/____/____

LESSON OBJECTIVE:

During this lesson, the instructor will introduce the student to en route IFR publications and procedures.

CONTENT:

Lesson Introduction

- _____ Airport / Facility Directory
- _____ VFR / IFR Low Altitude Planning Chart
- _____ En Route Low Altitude IFR Chart
- _____ En Route Chart Symbology
- _____ Air Traffic Service (ATS) Route System
- _____ Intersections and Changeover Points

Lesson Introduction

- _____ ATS Route Course Changes
- _____ Cockpit Management
- _____ Position Reporting Requirements
- _____ Additional Reporting Requirements
- _____ Loss of Communications Procedures (IMC and VMC)

COMPLETION STANDARDS:

At the completion of this lesson, the student will have an understanding of IFR navigation charts.

REQUIRED STUDY:

FAA-H-8261-1-IPH
FAA-H-8083-15-IFH
AIM
Instrument Rating Practical Test Standards
Vol 4: Segments 1-14

Notes:

STAGE III
LESSON 41
DUAL - GROUND
IFR CROSS-COUNTRY
PLANNING

DATE_____ GRADE (Circle One) S U I

STUDENT NAME _____ STUDENT SIGNATURE_____

INSTRUCTOR # _____ INSTRUCTOR SIGNATURE_____

DISCUSSION: (1.2) _____

CRS TOTALS: (F/I/D/FS) ____/____/____/____

LESSON OBJECTIVE:

During this lesson, the instructor will introduce the student to IFR cross-country flight planning.

CONTENT:

Lesson Introduction

_____ Charts & Publications
_____ Weather Briefing
_____ NOTAMs
_____ Determination of an Alternate
_____ Preferred IFR Routes
_____ DPs / STARs
_____ Takeoff Minimums

Lesson Introduction

_____ Cruising Altitudes
_____ Aircraft Performance
_____ Flight Plan Filing
_____ Cockpit Management
_____ Aeronautical Decision Making & Judgment
_____ Crew Resource Management

COMPLETION STANDARDS:

At the completion of this lesson, the student will be able to plan an IFR cross-country flight.

REQUIRED STUDY:

FAA-H-8083-15-IFH
AIM
Instrument Rating Practical Test Standards
Vol 4: Segments 1-6
Vol 7: Segments 5-14

Notes:

Sporty's *Complete* Flight Training Course — Stage III

STAGE III
LESSON 42
DUAL – FTD
CROSS-COUNTRY

DATE_____ ACFT/FTD ID_____ GRADE (Circle One) S U I

STUDENT NAME _____ STUDENT SIGNATURE_____

INSTRUCTOR # _____ INSTRUCTOR SIGNATURE_____

FTD/SIM: (2.0) _____   DISCUSSION: (0.4) _____

CRS TOTALS: (F/I/D/FS) ____/____/____/____

LESSON OBJECTIVE:

During this lesson, the instructor will introduce the student to IFR cross-country flight planning and review executing instrument approaches.

CONTENT:

Lesson Introduction

_____ En Route Navigation Including Lost Communications Procedures
_____ Dealing with En Route & Terminal Weather - Planning an Alternate
_____ Preparation of an IFR Navigation Log
_____ Planning Departures and Arrivals
_____ Power / Fuel Management

Lesson Review

_____ Copying / Understanding IFR Clearances
_____ Nonprecision Approach
_____ Precision Approach
_____ Missed Approach Procedures
_____ Circle to Land Procedures

COMPLETION STANDARDS:

At the completion of this lesson, the student will be able to plan an IFR cross-country flight and complete an IFR navigation log. The student will maintain headings ±5° en route/±10° on approaches, maintain altitudes, other than flight at MDA or during the final approach segment of a precision approach, ±100', maintain airspeeds ±10 knots, and maintain turning angles of bank ±5°. During nonprecision approaches the student will maintain the MDA, when reached, +100/-0 feet to the MAP and allow no more than a three-quarter-scale deflection of the CDI while on the final approach segment. During precision approaches the student will avoid descents below the DA/DH before initiating a missed approach procedure or transitioning to a normal landing approach and allow no more than a three-quarter-scale deflection of the localizer or glideslope while on the final approach segment

REQUIRED STUDY:

FAA-H-8083-15-IFH
Instrument Rating Practical Test Standards
Vol 4: Review Segments as Needed
Vol 6: Segments 1-5

Notes:

Stage III — *What You Should Know*

STAGE III
LESSON 43
DUAL - AIRCRAFT
     CROSS-COUNTRY

DATE_____ ACFT/FTD ID_____ GRADE (Circle One) S U I

STUDENT NAME _____ STUDENT SIGNATURE_____

INSTRUCTOR # _____ INSTRUCTOR SIGNATURE_____

FLIGHT TIME: (3.0) _____ DISCUSSION: (0.4) _____

INSTRUMENT: (2.8) _____ CRS TOTALS: (F/I/D/FS) ____/____/____/____

LESSON OBJECTIVE:

During this lesson, the instructor will review IFR cross-country flight planning and executing instrument approaches with the student. The cross-country should be planned to multiple airports with at least one airport more than 75 nautical miles from the departure airport. All airports should be sufficiently spaced to allow the student at least some realistic en route time.

CONTENT:

Lesson Introduction

_____ Dealing with En Route Weather
_____ Preparation of an IFR Navigation Log
_____ Planning Departures and Arrivals
_____ Power / Fuel Management

Lesson Review

_____ Filing an IFR Flight Plan
_____ Copying / Understanding IFR Clearances
_____ Nonprecision Approach
_____ APV Approach
_____ Precision Approach
_____ Missed Approach Procedures
_____ Circle to Land Procedures

COMPLETION STANDARDS:

At the completion of this lesson, the student will be able to perform an IFR cross-country with minimal assistance from the instructor. The student will maintain headings ±5° en route/±10° on approaches, maintain altitudes, other than flight at MDA or during the final approach segment of a precision approach, ±100', maintain airspeeds ±10 knots, and maintain turning angles of bank ±5°. During nonprecision approaches the student will maintain the MDA, when reached, +100/-0 feet to the MAP and allow no more than a three-quarter-scale deflection of the CDI while on the final approach segment. During precision approaches the student will avoid descents below the DA/DH before initiating a missed approach procedure or transitioning to a normal landing approach and allow no more than a three-quarter-scale deflection of the localizer or glideslope while on the final approach segment.

REQUIRED STUDY:

FAA-H-8083-15-IFH
Instrument Rating Practical Test Standards
Vol 2: Review Segments as Needed
Vol 3: Review Segments as Needed
Vol 5: Review Segments as Needed
Vol 6: Segments 6-10

Notes:
_____
_____
_____
_____
_____

STAGE III
LESSON 44
DUAL – FTD
CROSS-COUNTRY

DATE_____ ACFT/FTD ID_____ GRADE (Circle One) S U I

STUDENT NAME _____ STUDENT SIGNATURE_____

INSTRUCTOR # _____ INSTRUCTOR SIGNATURE_____

FTD/SIM: (2.0) _____ DISCUSSION: (0.4) _____

CRS TOTALS: (F/I/D/FS) ____/____/____/____

LESSON OBJECTIVE:

During this lesson, the instructor will review IFR cross-country flight planning and decision making and executing instrument approaches.

CONTENT:

Lesson Review

_____ Dealing with En Route & Terminal Weather
_____ Preparation of an IFR Navigation Log
_____ Planning Departures and Arrivals
_____ Lost Communications Procedures
_____ Copying / Understanding IFR Clearances

Lesson Review

_____ DME Arc
_____ Nonprecision Approach - Partial Panel
_____ Precision Approach
_____ Missed Approach Procedures
_____ Circle to Land Procedures

COMPLETION STANDARDS:

At the completion of this lesson, the student will be able to plan an IFR cross-country flight and complete an IFR navigation log. The student will maintain headings ±5° en route/±10° on approaches, maintain altitudes, other than flight at MDA or during the final approach segment of a precision approach, ±100', maintain airspeeds ±10 knots, and maintain turning angles of bank ±5°. During nonprecision approaches the student will maintain the MDA, when reached, +100/-0 feet to the MAP and allow no more than a three-quarter-scale deflection of the CDI while on the final approach segment. During precision approaches the student will avoid descents below the DA/DH before initiating a missed approach procedure or transitioning to a normal landing approach and allow no more than a three-quarter-scale deflection of the localizer or glideslope while on the final approach segment

REQUIRED STUDY:

FAA-H-8083-15-IFH
Instrument Rating Practical Test Standards
Vol 3: Segments 15-18
Vol 4: Review Segments as Needed

Notes:

STAGE III
LESSON 45
DUAL – AIRCRAFT
    CROSS-COUNTRY

DATE_____ ACFT/FTD ID_____ GRADE (Circle One) S U I

STUDENT NAME _____ STUDENT SIGNATURE_____

INSTRUCTOR # _____ INSTRUCTOR SIGNATURE_____

FLIGHT TIME: (4.0) _____ DISCUSSION: (0.4) _____

INSTRUMENT: (3.8) _____ CRS TOTALS: (F/I/D/FS) ___/___/___/___

LESSON OBJECTIVE:

During this lesson, the instructor will review IFR cross-country flight planning and executing instrument approaches with the student. **The student will also perform a cross-country flight of at least 250 nautical miles along airways or an ATC-directed routing with one segment of the flight consisting of at least a straight-line distance of 100 nautical miles between airports; involving an instrument approach at each airport; and involving three different kinds of approaches with the use of navigation systems.** The autopilot should be used where appropriate to assist in management of the aircraft.

CONTENT:

Lesson Review

_____ Filing an IFR Flight Plan
_____ Copying / Understanding IFR Clearances
_____ Dealing with En Route Weather
_____ Preparation of an IFR Navigation Log
_____ Planning Departures and Arrivals
_____ Power / Fuel Management

Lesson Review

_____ Nonprecision Approach
_____ Precision Approach
_____ Missed Approach Procedures
_____ Approaches with an Autopilot (Precision & Nonprecision)
_____ Circle to Land Procedures

COMPLETION STANDARDS:

At the completion of this lesson, the student will be able to perform an IFR cross-country with minimal assistance from the instructor. The student will utilize the autopilot as appropriate to assist in managing the aircraft but will not display dependence on it. The student will maintain headings ±5° en route/±10° on approaches, maintain altitudes, other than flight at MDA or during the final approach segment of a precision approach, ±100', maintain airspeeds ±10 knots, and maintain turning angles of bank ±5°. During nonprecision approaches the student will maintain the MDA, when reached, +100/-0 feet to the MAP and allow no more than a three-quarter-scale deflection of the CDI while on the final approach segment. During precision approaches the student will avoid descents below the DA/DH before initiating a missed approach procedure or transitioning to a normal landing approach and allow no more than a three-quarter-scale deflection of the localizer or glideslope while on the final approach segment

REQUIRED STUDY:

FAA-H-8083-15-IFH
Instrument Rating Practical Test Standards
Vol 4: Review Segments as Needed
Vol 6: Review Segments as Needed

Notes:

Sporty's *Complete* Flight Training Course — Stage III

STAGE III
LESSON 46
DUAL - GROUND
END OF STAGE REVIEW

DATE _____ GRADE (Circle One) S U I
STUDENT NAME _____ STUDENT SIGNATURE _____
INSTRUCTOR # _____ INSTRUCTOR SIGNATURE _____
DISCUSSION: (1.2) _____
CRS TOTALS: (F/I/D/FS) ____ / ____ / ____

LESSON OBJECTIVE:

The objective of this lesson is to evaluate the student's comprehension of the material presented in the Instrument Pilot Certification ground lessons.

CONTENT:

Lesson Review

_____ Instrument Pilot Knowledge Test
_____ Weather Information
_____ Cross-Country Flight Planning
_____ Aircraft Systems Related to IFR Flight

Lesson Review

_____ Aircraft Flight / Navigation Equipment
_____ Instrument Cockpit Check
_____ FARs Related to IFR Flight

COMPLETION STANDARDS:

In order to complete the ground portion of the Instrument Pilot Certification Course, the student must score at least a 70% on the Instrument Pilot Knowledge Test. The student must have instrument pilot level knowledge of the items listed for review.

Notes:

Stage III *What You Should Know*

STAGE III
LESSON 47
DUAL - AIRCRAFT
END OF STAGE REVIEW

DATE_____ ACFT/FTD ID_____ GRADE (Circle One) S U I

STUDENT NAME _____ STUDENT SIGNATURE_____

INSTRUCTOR # _____ INSTRUCTOR SIGNATURE_____

FLIGHT TIME: (2.0) _____ DISCUSSION: (0.4) _____

INSTRUMENT: (1.8) _____ CRS TOTALS: (F/I/D/FS) ____/____/____/____

LESSON OBJECTIVE:

During this lesson, the instructor will review instrument flight procedures with the student in preparation for the final stage check.

CONTENT:

Lesson Review

_____ Instrument Cockpit Check
_____ ATC Clearances & Communications
_____ Compliance with Departure, En Route, and Arrival Procedures and Clearances
_____ Holding Procedures
_____ Basic Instrument Flight Maneuvers
_____ Partial Panel Instrument Flight
_____ Steep Turns
_____ Recovery from Unusual Attitudes
_____ Intercepting / Tracking Navigation Systems
_____ Nonprecision Approach - Full Approach
_____ Nonprecision Approach - Vectored
_____ Nonprecision Approach with an Autopilot

Lesson Review

_____ Nonprecision Approach with Loss of Primary Flight Instrument Indicators
_____ APV Approach
_____ Precision Approach
_____ Missed Approach Procedures
_____ Missed Approach Procedures with an Autopilot
_____ Circling Approach
_____ Landing from Straight-In / Circling Approaches
_____ Loss of Communications
_____ Checking Instruments and Equipment

COMPLETION STANDARDS:

The student shall perform all maneuvers to the standards established by the Instrument Rating Practical Test Standards.

REQUIRED STUDY:

FAA-H-8083-15-IFH
Instrument Rating Practical Test Standards
Vol 7: Segments 1-14

Note: The Nonprecision Approach with Loss of Primary Flight Instrument Indicators and the Nonprecision Approach with an Autopilot can be combined with the full and vectored approaches. Just as the practical test standards require, the student should complete at least 2 nonprecision approaches and 1 precision approach during this review session. At least 1 nonprecision approach should include a procedure turn or a full TAA transition. An APV approach may be substituted for one of the nonprecision approaches if so equipped. While this review flight can be flown as a practice checkride, it is important to ensure that the student is fully prepared for any type of approach that the airplane is capable of flying prior to the checkride thus additional approaches may be appropriate.

Notes:
_____
_____
_____
_____
_____

Sporty's *Complete* Flight Training Course — Stage II

PRE-STAGE CHECK – TIME SUMMARY

This page is intended to be used by the student's flight instructor to summarize the times accumulated through this course of instruction and determine that the times are sufficient for the stage requirements. The check instructor should verify that these times are acceptable for completion of the stage.

Part 141 Note: The instrument time in an approved FTD used to meet the minimum requirements of Part 141 may not exceed 40% of the total instrument time required for the course of instruction. This limit is raised to 50% for an approved flight simulator or a combination of an FTD and a simulator.

DATE_____ STUDENT NAME _____ STUDENT SIGNATURE_____

INSTRUCTOR # _____ INSTRUCTOR SIGNATURE_____

STAGE TOTALS

FLIGHT TIME: _____ (In stage only.)

GROUND/DISCUSSION: _____ (Be sure to include the Ground Lesson times.)

FTD/SIM: _____ (In stage only.)

INSTRUMENT: _____ (In flight only.)

COURSE TOTALS

FLIGHT TIME: _____ (In course only.)

GROUND/DISCUSSION: _____ (Be sure to include the Ground Lesson times.)

FTD/SIM: _____ (In course only.)

INSTRUMENT: _____ (In flight only.)

Stage III   *What You Should Know*

STAGE III
LESSON 48
STAGE III CHECK

DATE_____ ACFT/FTD ID_____ GRADE (Circle One) S U I

STUDENT NAME _____ STUDENT SIGNATURE_____

INSTRUCTOR # _____ INSTRUCTOR SIGNATURE_____

FLIGHT TIME: (2.0) _____ DISCUSSION: (1.0) _____

LESSON OBJECTIVE:

INSTRUMENT: (1.8) _____ CRS TOTALS: (F/I/D/FS) ____/____/____/____

During this lesson, the student will complete a stage check for the Instrument Rating.

CONTENT:

Lesson Review

ORAL
_____ Weather Information
_____ Cross-Country Flight Planning
_____ Aircraft Systems Related to IFR Flight
_____ Aircraft Flight / Navigation Equipment
_____ Instrument Cockpit Check
_____ FARs Related to IFR Flight

FLIGHT
_____ Instrument Cockpit Check
_____ ATC Clearances
_____ Compliance with Departure, En Route, and Arrival Procedures and Clearances
_____ Holding Procedures
_____ Basic Instrument Flight Maneuvers
_____ Partial Panel Instrument Flight
_____ Steep Turns
_____ Recovery from Unusual Attitudes

Lesson Review

FLIGHT (continued)
_____ Intercepting / Tracking Navigation Systems
_____ Nonprecision Approach - Full Approach
_____ Nonprecision Approach - Vectored
_____ Nonprecision Approach with an Autopilot
_____ Nonprecision Approach with Loss of Primary Flight Instrument Indicators
_____ APV Approach
_____ Precision Approach
_____ Missed Approach Procedures
_____ Missed Approach Procedures with an Autopilot
_____ Circling Approach
_____ Landing from Straight-In / Circling Approaches
_____ Loss of Communications
_____ Checking Instruments and Equipment

COMPLETION STANDARDS:

The student shall perform all maneuvers to the standards established by the Instrument Rating Practical Test Standards.

REQUIRED STUDY:

Instrument Rating Practical Test Standards
Vol 1-7: Review Segments as Needed

Note: The Nonprecision Approach with Loss of Primary Flight Instrument Indicators and the Nonprecision Approach with an Autopilot can be combined with the full and vectored approaches. Just as the practical test standards require, the student should complete at least 2 nonprecision approaches and 1 precision approach during this stage check. At least 1 nonprecision approach should include a procedure turn or a full TAA transition. An APV approach may be substituted for one of the nonprecision approaches if so equipped.

Notes:
_____
_____
_____
_____
_____

RECORD OF EXTRA TRAINING

DATE_____ ACFT/FTD ID_____ GRADE (Circle One) S U I

STUDENT NAME _____ STUDENT SIGNATURE_____

INSTRUCTOR # _____ INSTRUCTOR SIGNATURE_____

FLIGHT TIME: _____ DISCUSSION: _____

CRS TOTALS: (F/I/D/FS) ____/____/____/____

CONTENT:

RECORD OF EXTRA TRAINING

DATE_____ ACFT/FTD ID_____ GRADE (Circle One) S U I

STUDENT NAME _____ STUDENT SIGNATURE_____

INSTRUCTOR # _____ INSTRUCTOR SIGNATURE_____

FLIGHT TIME: _____ DISCUSSION: _____

CRS TOTALS: (F/I/D/FS) ____/____/____/____

CONTENT:

RECORD OF EXTRA TRAINING

DATE_____ ACFT/FTD ID_____ GRADE (Circle One) S U I

STUDENT NAME _____ STUDENT SIGNATURE_____

INSTRUCTOR # _____ INSTRUCTOR SIGNATURE_____

FLIGHT TIME: _____ DISCUSSION: _____

CRS TOTALS: (F/I/D/FS) ____/____/____/____

CONTENT:

RECORD OF EXTRA TRAINING

DATE_____ ACFT/FTD ID_____ GRADE (Circle One) S U I

STUDENT NAME _____ STUDENT SIGNATURE_____

INSTRUCTOR # _____ INSTRUCTOR SIGNATURE_____

FLIGHT TIME: _____ DISCUSSION: _____

CRS TOTALS: (F/I/D/FS) ____/____/____/____

CONTENT:

RECORD OF EXTRA TRAINING

DATE_____ ACFT/FTD ID_____ GRADE (Circle One) S U I

STUDENT NAME _____ STUDENT SIGNATURE_____

INSTRUCTOR # _____ INSTRUCTOR SIGNATURE_____

FLIGHT TIME: _____ DISCUSSION: _____

CRS TOTALS: (F/I/D/FS) ____/____/____/____

CONTENT:

RECORD OF EXTRA TRAINING

DATE_____ ACFT/FTD ID_____ GRADE (Circle One) S U I

STUDENT NAME _____ STUDENT SIGNATURE_____

INSTRUCTOR # _____ INSTRUCTOR SIGNATURE_____

FLIGHT TIME: _____ DISCUSSION: _____

CRS TOTALS: (F/I/D/FS) ____/____/____/____

CONTENT:

RECORD OF EXTRA TRAINING

DATE _____ ACFT/FTD ID _____ GRADE (Circle One) S U I

STUDENT NAME _____ STUDENT SIGNATURE _____

INSTRUCTOR # _____ INSTRUCTOR SIGNATURE _____

FLIGHT TIME: _____ DISCUSSION: _____

CRS TOTALS: (F/I/D/FS) ____ /____ /____ /____

CONTENT: